P9-BZI-166

new vegetarian
entertaining

new vegetarian **entertaining**

simply spectacular recipes

Jane Noraika

with photography by **william lingwood**

RYLAND
PETERS
& SMALL

LONDON NEW YORK

Dedication

Mum, with love and thanks

First published in the United States in 2003
by Ryland Peters & Small, Inc.
519 Broadway, 5th Floor, New York, NY 10012
www.rylandpeters.com

Text © Jane Noraika 2003
Design and photographs
© Ryland Peters & Small 2003

10 9 8 7 6 5 4 3 2 1

The author's moral rights have been
asserted. All rights reserved. No part of this
publication may be reproduced, stored in a
retrieval system, or transmitted in any form
or by any means, electronic, mechanical,
photocopying, or otherwise, without the
prior permission of the publisher.

Library of Congress Cataloging-in-
Publication Data

Noraika, Jane.

  New vegetarian entertaining : simply
spectacular recipes / Jane Noraika ; with
photography by William Lingwood.

     p. cm.

  ISBN 1-84172-418-1

  1. Vegetarian cookery. 2. Entertaining.
I. Title.

  TX837 .N58 2002

  641.5'636--dc21

                          2002151165

Printed and bound in China.

Commissioning Editor
Elsa Petersen-Schepelern
Editors
Kim Davies,
Jennifer Herman Clair
Production
Patricia Harrington
Art Director
Gabriella Le Grazie
Publishing Director
Alison Starling

Food Stylist
Joss Herd
Stylist
Antonia Gaunt
Indexer
Hilary Bird
Photographer's Assistant
Emma Bentham-Wood

NOTES

All spoon measurements
are level unless otherwise
stated.

All eggs are large unless
otherwise stated.

All fruits and vegetables
should be washed
thoroughly and peeled,
unless otherwise stated.
Unwaxed citrus fruits
should be used whenever
the zest will be used.
When unavailable, the
fruit should be washed in
warm water.

Skillets, ovens, and grills
should be preheated to
the required temperature—
if using a convection oven,
cooking times should be
reduced according to the
manufacturer's
instructions.

Specialty Asian
ingredients are available
in large supermarkets,
Thai, Chinese, and
Asian stores.

Author's Acknowledgments

I would like to thank everyone who
made the experience of producing this
book so rewarding, satisfying, and, in
particular, fun. I would like to single out
Mel Barrett for her enthusiasm and ideas
while testing some recipes with me,
particularly on the Sunday Lunch section.
Also Gabi Matzeu for sharing a few of
his family's Italian secrets. A big thank
you to Joss and William for working their
magic on creating and photographing
the food. It was a pleasure to share my
house for ten days with them when they
were doing this. A big thank you to
everyone at Ryland Peters & Small.

contents

introduction

Oh the joys of cooking! Everywhere we go or wherever we look, our tastebuds are bombarded by images of food. There they are on TV showing us how to produce a three-course meal at supersonic speed, and in magazine or newspaper articles instructing us on what we should be eating, how to cook it, and, what's more, which "trendy" ingredients we should be using. We are further seduced by the wondrous array of materials available in supermarkets, and in specialty and gourmet stores. Never before has there been so much pressure on the cook to produce amazing varied food, effortlessly and joyfully. And then a vegetarian shows up ...

You are already pushed to your limit on time and creative ability, and feel that the evening is going to be spent in lonely solitude in the kitchen with only the oven as company.

My aim with *New Vegetarian Entertaining* is for you to take a sigh of relief and relax. It is possible to produce amazing food, even for a lot of people, and spend time with those you really want to- your guests. As the host, the objective is to do as much as possible in advance, taking any last-minute strain out of the occasion, and making sure that your guests are greeted by the aromas of beautiful home-cooked food when they arrive.

There are chapters in this book for various social settings with dishes to suit each one. When your vegetarian friend appears, rather than your heart sinking, it should be a time to impress all your guests, whether they're vegetarian or not. When I cater for large private parties, I love it when a guest comments, in surprise, at the end of the party that they didn't even notice that no meat was used. Vegetarian food has long come out of the wilderness years of nut roasts and cutlets. Now, more than ever, with the multitude of cosmopolitan ingredients at our disposal, plus organic produce and farmers' markets springing up everywhere, it is possible to produce modern, clean-tasting food that is easy on the eye and will sit effortlessly alongside meat and fish, allowing vegetarians to blend in with the crowd.

FINGERFOOD

herb and feta polenta

topped with sun-dried tomato tapenade

These Italian polenta (cornmeal) rounds are a dream for any party because everything can be made in advance—in fact, if you are super-organized you can make the tapenade several weeks ahead. When serving polenta firm, it is always better to leave it overnight to set. You can cut it up and top with the tapenade a few hours before the party. Bring out the colors by serving on a bed of greens such as lamb's lettuce (mâche), arugula, or watercress.

3 tablespoons unsalted butter

1 tablespoon olive oil

1 garlic clove, crushed

3 scallions, finely chopped

1/4 cup plus 2 tablespoons polenta or yellow cornmeal, about 2 oz.

4 oz. feta cheese, crumbled into small pieces

a small handful of dill, coarsely chopped

sea salt and freshly ground black pepper

8–16 pitted black olives, sliced, to serve

TOMATO TAPENADE

2 oz. sun-dried tomatoes, soaked overnight in warm water with 1 tablespoon vinegar

1/3 cup olive oil

1 tablespoon balsamic vinegar

1/2 red serrano chile, seeded

a small handful of basil leaves

a baking pan, 8-inches square, well greased

a cookie cutter, 2-inches diameter

MAKES 16

To make the tapenade, put the soaked tomatoes in a blender with the olive oil, balsamic vinegar, chile, and basil. Process until fairly smooth.

To make the polenta, put the butter, oil, garlic, and scallions in a saucepan and cook for 10 minutes until the onions are translucent. Pour in 1 1/4 cups boiling water, then add the polenta in a steady stream, whisking all the time to stop lumps forming. Continue cooking according to the instructions on the polenta package. Stir in the feta and dill, add salt and pepper to taste, then pour into the prepared pan. Chill in the refrigerator overnight.

Cut out 16 rounds with the cookie cutter. Top each round with a generous spoonful of tapenade and a few slices of black olives, then serve.

COOK'S TIP

To store the tapenade, put in a screw-top bottle and cover with a thin layer of olive oil. Keep in the refrigerator for 2–3 weeks. The tapenade also makes a good crostini topping or a pasta sauce.

1 baguette loaf,
thinly sliced

olive oil, for brushing

GUACAMOLE

2 ripe avocados, peeled
and seeds removed

1 tomato, quartered,
seeded, and finely
chopped

1/2 red onion, very finely
chopped

freshly squeezed juice
of 1 lime

1/2 garlic clove, crushed

1 teaspoon olive oil

sea salt and freshly
ground black pepper

coarsely chopped
cilantro, to serve

a baking tray

MAKES 12

crostini with guacamole

There are lots of different tricks used to prevent avocado from discoloring. Some of the more successful ones are to use citrus juice, to cover the bowl with plastic wrap, or to leave an avocado seed in the guacamole until you are ready to serve. To make absolutely sure of a good color, avoid making the dip too far in advance, and if possible serve it as soon as it's made. That shouldn't be difficult—this dish is hard to resist!

Brush both sides of the bread with olive oil and put on the baking tray. Toast in a preheated oven at 400°F for 5 minutes on each side until crisp and lightly golden.

Meanwhile, to make the guacamole, put the avocado in a bowl and mash with a fork until fairly smooth. Stir in the tomato, red onion, lime juice, garlic, and olive oil. Add salt and pepper to taste.

Top each toasted slice with a generous spoonful of guacamole, then serve with cilantro on top.

baby tomatoes

filled with pesto risotto

Be warned, if you are using cherry tomatoes this can be fiddly and a little time-consuming. However, I have made them for seventy and survived! When using larger tomatoes, provide your guests with plates or be prepared for a major clean-up operation. For a hassle-free approach, make the risotto and scoop out the insides of the tomatoes a day ahead, then fill them before your guests arrive. This dish is well worth the trouble, and the combination of tomato and basil is always a big hit.

Using a small, sharp knife, slice off the stalk end of each tomato and reserve. To make sure the tomatoes sit squarely on a plate, slice off the pointed bases. Using a teaspoon, scoop out the insides and turn upside-down to drain out any excess juices.

Melt the butter in a saucepan, then add the olive oil and garlic. Add the onion and cook for 10 minutes until softened. Add the rice, stirring to absorb the buttery juices. Add the stock a ladle at a time, stirring frequently, and letting the rice absorb the liquid between each addition—about 15 minutes. Stir in the pesto, add salt and pepper to taste, then let cool.

Using a teaspoon, fill each tomato with risotto. Press the reserved lids on top at a jaunty angle, then serve.

16 baby tomatoes, preferably on the vine

2 tablespoons unsalted butter

1 tablespoon olive oil

1 garlic clove, crushed

1/2 white onion, finely chopped

1/3 cup risotto rice, such as arborio

1 1/4 cups vegetable stock or hot water

1 tablespoon prepared pesto

sea salt and freshly ground black pepper

MAKES 16

garlic croutons
with camembert and caramelized onion

A sophisticated French take on the very popular cheese on toast!

1 baguette loaf,
thinly sliced

1 tablespoon olive oil,
plus extra for brushing

1 garlic clove

1 onion, quartered,
then thinly sliced

1 teaspoon brown sugar

a pinch of salt

4 oz. Camembert cheese,
thinly sliced

sprigs of thyme, to serve

a baking tray

MAKES 12

Put the slices of bread on the baking tray and lightly brush each side with olive oil. Toast in a preheated oven at 400°F until both sides are lightly golden. Rub the garlic clove over one or both sides of the toast, depending on how much you love garlic.

Meanwhile, heat the 1 tablespoon oil in a saucepan, add the onion, and cook gently for 10 minutes until softened. Stir in the sugar and a pinch of salt.

Put a thin slice of Camembert on each crouton, then pile the onion mixture on top. Serve topped with a tiny sprig of thyme.

COOK'S TIP

I love the flavor of garlic, but it can easily dominate a dish if you use too much. A good rule to remember is that the less garlic is cut or crushed, the stronger the flavor will be. In this recipe a whole uncut clove is being rubbed over the toast, so moderation is required.

tandoori tofu

These succulent, spicy morsels are original enough to surprise any guest. Be sure to make plenty of them since they make for very compulsive eating. Wonderful with cocktails.

Cut the tofu into bite-size pieces and put into a large bowl.

Put the yogurt into another bowl, add the tomato paste, garlic, ginger, chile, salt, and toasted cumin and coriander seeds, and stir well. Spoon the mixture over the tofu and toss gently so that each piece is well coated. Set aside to marinate in the refrigerator for at least 1 hour.

Spread over a roasting tray and cook in a preheated oven at 400°F for 40 minutes, stirring halfway through the cooking time.

Transfer to a platter, then sprinkle with the lemon juice and cilantro.

Let your guests help themselves to these succulent pieces of tofu, using a cocktail stick. Alternatively, thread a tiny wedge of lemon onto each stick, followed by a tofu cube.

COOK'S TIPS

The best way to store fresh ginger is in the freezer. Using a fine grater, grate as much of the frozen ginger as you need with no peeling or waste.

To be super-organized, marinate the tofu overnight in the refrigerator.

1¼ lb. deep-fried tofu, cut into bite-size pieces

¾ cup thick Greek-style yogurt, about 6 oz.

2 tablespoons tomato purée

1 garlic clove, crushed

1 inch fresh ginger, grated

1 green serrano chile, finely chopped, including seeds

1 teaspoon cumin seeds, lightly toasted in a dry skillet and ground in a coffee grinder

2 teaspoons coriander seeds, lightly toasted in a dry skillet and ground in a coffee grinder

1 teaspoon sea salt

freshly squeezed juice of ½ lemon

coarsely chopped cilantro, to serve

a baking tray

cocktail sticks

MAKES ABOUT 12

smoky spanish tortilla

1 lb. potatoes, cut into large pieces

1 tablespoon olive oil

7 scallions, thinly sliced

⅓ teaspoon Spanish smoked paprika

1 garlic clove, crushed

½ red serrano chile, seeded and finely chopped

6 eggs, lightly beaten

sea salt and freshly ground black pepper

a non-stick skillet, 9-inches diameter

MAKES ABOUT 30

This delicious variation of the classic Spanish omelet includes the rather potent addition of smoked paprika. It works well as part of a fingerfood selection because it's fairly filling—and so helps prevent your guests from getting too merry too quickly! For the best results, make it on the same day as you are going to serve it. This tortilla also makes a delicious rustic lunch—try it sandwiched between two pieces of crusty bread with just a little mayonnaise.

Cook the potatoes for 15 minutes in plenty of boiling, salted water. When tender, drain through a colander and let cool before cutting into smaller pieces.

Put the oil in the skillet. Add the scallions, paprika, garlic, and chile and cook for 5 minutes until the onion has softened.

Add salt and pepper to the beaten eggs, then stir in the cooked potatoes. Add the mixture to the pan. Keep the eggs moving in the pan until they start to set, then continue to cook the tortilla for a few more minutes,

keeping the heat low. Invert the tortilla onto a plate, then slide back into the pan, uncooked side down. Cook for a further 3–4 minutes before sliding onto a plate (the center of the tortilla should still be a little soft).

Let cool slightly, then cut into about 30 diamond-shaped pieces or serve in larger wedges.

COOK'S TIP

Add some spinach, black olives, and freshly chopped dill for a Greek-style tortilla.

pumpernickel squares

with cream cheese, horseradish, and beets

People either love or hate beets—I definitely fall into the "love them" category. I enjoy making these delicious bites because they look divine. When preparing fingerfood, the aesthetics are very important, and beet lends its magnificent color. You may even recruit a few converts along the way!

⅔ cup cream cheese, about 6 oz.

1 tablespoon horseradish

8 oz. (about 6 slices) pumpernickel, each slice cut into 4 squares

3 oz. cooked beets (with no vinegar), sliced thinly into rounds, about 1 cup

4 pickles, thinly sliced

2 hard-cooked eggs, finely chopped

fresh dill, coarsely chopped, to serve

MAKES ABOUT 24

Mix the cream cheese and horseradish in a bowl, then spread over the squares of pumpernickel. Top with a slice of beet, then a slice of pickle, some chopped hard-cooked egg, and fresh dill.

COOK'S TIPS

You can buy precooked beets in some supermarkets, freshly cooked or in jars. To cook beets yourself, either roast or boil them, unpeeled. Take care not to damage the skins—don't trim them, just cut off the leaves about 1 inch from the beet. To roast them, cook in a preheated oven at 400°F until tender (the time will depend on the size of the beets—test them with a skewer). If boiling beets, simmer in a large saucepan of salted water until done (as above), then drain, let cool a little, then slip off the skins.

As a variation, use squares of rye toast instead of pumpernickel.

Roast some halved walnuts with a little cayenne pepper and soy sauce. Let cool, then use to top the beets—omit the pickle and egg. Finish with a thin slice of apple.

wild mushroom and almond moneybags

Creamy-textured ground almonds are a wonderful alternative to the less exciting bread crumbs that are often used to stuff mushrooms. The slight sweetness of the almonds is a magnificent complement to the rich meatiness of wild mushrooms.

1 tablespoon olive oil, plus extra for brushing

½ teaspoon paprika

1 lb. mixed mushrooms, thinly sliced

3 scallions, finely chopped

a bunch of flat-leaf parsley, finely chopped

2 tablespoons ground almonds

1 teaspoon lemon juice

sea salt and freshly ground black pepper

8 oz. phyllo pastry dough, thawed if frozen (half a 16 oz. package)

a baking tray, lightly greased

MAKES 8

Put the olive oil, paprika, mushrooms, and scallions in a large skillet, then cook for 10–15 minutes until the mushrooms are tender and start to release their liquid. Stir in the parsley, ground almonds, lemon juice, salt, and pepper.

If the dough isn't already rolled, roll it out to about ⅛ inch thick. Cut the sheets of dough into 6-inch squares. Keeping the others covered with a damp cloth while you work, put a sheet of phyllo on a work surface and brush lightly with olive oil. Put another square of dough on top and lightly brush again with oil.

Put a spoonful of mushroom mixture in the center. Pull the edges of the dough up to the middle, twist to seal, then put on the prepared baking tray. Repeat to make 8 moneybags.

Bake in a preheated oven at 350°F for 20 minutes until lightly golden brown (if the tops brown too quickly, cover loosely with foil to stop them burning).

COOK'S TIPS

For a great entrée, make larger moneybags and serve with roasted tomatoes and a selection of vegetables.

If you can't find ground almonds in the baking section of the supermarket, use slivered almonds and grind them yourself using a small blender or a mortar and pestle.

roasted red bell pepper and goat cheese rolls

These rolls are a fabulous addition to any array of fingerfood. They may seem slightly complicated, but there are many ways to make life simpler: buy the tapenade or make it up a couple of weeks in advance, roast and peel the peppers the night before, then assemble the rolls well in advance. These are a real treat for the tastebuds, with sweet, tart, and salty flavors in one mouthful. The vibrant red of the pepper is also very alluring.

Put the bell peppers on the baking tray and sprinkle with olive oil. Roast in a preheated oven at 425°F for about 30 minutes until charred and blistered. Remove from the oven and cover with a damp dish towel. Set aside for 5–10 minutes to steam off the skins—this makes peeling much easier.

Meanwhile, to make the olive tapenade, put the olives, olive oil, and capers in a blender and process to a fairly coarse mixture.

Carefully remove the skins from the bell peppers, making sure you don't tear the flesh, then cut each half in half again. Put each piece of pepper, skinned side down, on a work surface, then smear generously with the tapenade. Add a small piece of goat cheese and a few basil leaves. Carefully roll up the filled pepper, then put seam side down on a serving platter. Secure with a sprig of rosemary, if using, then serve.

COOK'S TIPS

Don't overfill the peppers—any remaining tapenade can be put in a screw-top bottle, covered with a thin layer of olive oil, and stored in the refrigerator for 2–3 weeks.

The rosemary skewers not only look good, but they also flavor the peppers.

4 red bell peppers, halved, seeded, and white membranes removed

olive oil, for sprinkling

6 oz. goat cheese, soft or firm, but not hard

a handful of fresh basil leaves

sprigs of rosemary, to serve (optional)

OLIVE TAPENADE

1 cup black olives, such as Niçoise or Kalamata, pitted

¼ cup olive oil

2 tablespoons capers, rinsed and drained

a baking tray

MAKES 16

eggplant party rolls
filled with mozzarella and sun-dried tomatoes

These rolls look beautiful as part of a fingerfood selection. The real delight is that the flavor improves if they are made the day before—which, of course, leaves you free to concentrate on other things. Make plenty, since they will be devoured very quickly.

2 medium eggplant, cut into about 18 thin slices

olive oil, for brushing

sea salt

½ jar of basil pesto (not all of this will be used)

2 oz. sun-dried tomatoes, soaked overnight in warm water with 1 tablespoon vinegar, then sliced into strips

4 oz. mozzarella cheese, cut into small strips

salad leaves such as arugula or radicchio, to serve

a baking tray

MAKES 36

Set the eggplant slices on the baking tray, brush with olive oil, then lightly sprinkle with salt. Roast in a preheated oven at 400°F for about 30 minutes or until tender. Remove from the oven and let cool slightly.

Spread each slice of eggplant with pesto. Add a slice of tomato and a strip of mozzarella. Roll up, then put seam side down on a serving platter. (The rolls look prettier if a little cheese and tomato tumbles out of the ends.)

Serve on salad leaves.

COOK'S TIP

I prefer the unhydrated variety of sun-dried tomatoes because I am outraged by the exorbitant prices of those packed in oil. It is so easy to hydrate the tomatoes yourself and it requires just a little planning.

8 oz. strawberries, stems on

8 oz. cherries, stems on

1 oz. milk chocolate, broken into small pieces

1 oz. white chocolate, broken into small pieces

1 oz. dark chocolate, broken into small pieces

wax paper

mini muffin paper liners

SERVES 4

strawberries and cherries
in tricolor chocolate

A truly seductive end to any party, these fruits make for a great finale.

Divide the strawberries and cherries into 3 equal piles.

Put the milk chocolate into a clean, dry, heatproof bowl and set over a saucepan of gently simmering water. Do not let the water touch the base of the bowl, or any water touch the chocolate, or the chocolate will seize and be unusable.

Take one of the piles of fruit and dip them halfway into the chocolate, leaving the tops and stems uncoated and visible. Transfer to a sheet of wax paper to set.

Repeat with the white and dark chocolate, and the other two piles of fruit. Chill for at least 1 hour.

To serve, peel off the wax paper and put a selection of fruit in a mini muffin paper liner. Alternatively, pile the fruit onto a large serving plate and invite your guests to help themselves.

COOK'S TIP

You must use a clean, dry bowl for each kind of chocolate, or the chocolate will be spoiled.

LITTLE MEALS AND TAPAS

sesame sweet potato wedges
with peanut dipping sauce

If, like me, you love the goodness of peanuts but cannot face peanut butter, you'll really appreciate this dipping sauce. It works superbly with the sweetness of the potato, which can be either roasted or deep-fried. Wonderful served with very cold beer.

Arrange the sweet potato wedges in a single layer on the baking tray, then sprinkle with the olive and sesame oils, sesame seeds, and salt. Roast in a preheated oven at 400°F for 35 minutes or until tender (the cooking time will vary depending on the size of the wedges).

Meanwhile, to prepare the dipping sauce, put the peanut butter, lime juice, chile, soy sauce, and tomato ketchup in a food processor, add $\frac{1}{4}$ cup hot water and blend until smooth. Add salt and pepper to taste, then pour into a saucepan and heat gently.

Sprinkle the wedges with the cilantro and serve with a separate bowl of the dipping sauce.

COOK'S TIP

To simplify this recipe even further, serve the wedges with store-bought sweet chile sauce.

1½ lb. sweet potatoes, about 4, well scrubbed but unpeeled, cut lengthwise into thick wedges

2 tablespoons olive oil

1 tablespoon toasted sesame oil

1 tablespoon sesame seeds

sea salt

coarsely torn or chopped cilantro, to serve

DIPPING SAUCE

2 tablespoons organic peanut butter

1 tablespoon lime juice

½ red serrano chile, seeded and sliced

1 tablespoon soy sauce

1 tablespoon tomato ketchup

sea salt and freshly ground black pepper

a baking tray

SERVES 6–8

saffron chickpeas

This is a wholly Italian recipe using ingredients that most Italians have in abundance in their kitchens. It is amazing how these few humble items are totally transformed by the scented elegance of saffron, bringing a touch of class to the dish.

2 tablespoons olive oil

1 onion, finely chopped

2 cups dried chickpeas, about 14 oz., soaked overnight, drained and cooked for 1–1½ hours (reserve some of the cooking liquid to use in the recipe)

3 large tomatoes, about 1 lb., peeled and chopped

2 garlic cloves, crushed

1¼ cups chickpea cooking liquid (see above)

a small pinch of saffron threads

sea salt and freshly ground black pepper

SERVES 4

Heat the oil in a large saucepan, add the onion, and cook for 10 minutes until translucent. Stir in the drained chickpeas, tomatoes, and garlic. Cook for 5 minutes, stirring occasionally.

Add the chickpea cooking liquid and bring to a boil, then reduce the heat and simmer for 25 minutes. Stir in the saffron and cook for a further 5 minutes. Add salt and pepper to taste, then serve.

COOK'S TIPS

Saffron is produced by drying the stigmas of certain varieties of crocus. Only 3 stigmas per flower can be harvested, making saffron an expensive spice, but worth every penny.

Dried beans are infinitely better than the canned varieties, which often have extra salt and sugar added—they are also much cheaper to buy. This recipe in particular should not be attempted with anything other than dried chickpeas, or it will be a mere shadow of the original dish.

couscous tabbouleh

One of my favorite salads. Don't be alarmed at the small quantity of couscous used—the salad is traditionally made mainly with herbs and vegetables and just a smattering of bulghar wheat. Couscous, a fine pasta from Morocco, is an easy alternative, very nutritious and light.

Put the couscous in a bowl with ⅓ cup cold water—enough to make the couscous just moist rather than saturated. Leave for 10 minutes or until fluffy. When ready, stir in the scallions, cucumber, tomatoes, parsley, and mint.

To make the lemon dressing, put the lemon juice, garlic, and olive oil in a bowl and beat with a fork. Stir into the salad, add salt and pepper to taste, then serve.

COOK'S TIP

I always like to use cold water to hydrate couscous, rather than using boiling water or steaming it. It still fluffs up well, but also retains an interesting al dente *texture, which I much prefer.*

⅓ cup couscous

4 scallions,
finely chopped

⅓ cucumber, cut into
very small cubes

3 tomatoes, about 10 oz.,
seeded then cut into
small cubes

a large handful of fresh
flat-leaf parsley leaves,
finely chopped (about
2 cups)

a small handful of fresh
mint leaves, finely
chopped (about ¾ cup)

LEMON DRESSING

freshly squeezed juice
of 1 lemon

1 garlic clove, crushed

3 tablespoons olive oil

sea salt and freshly
ground black pepper

SERVES 4

olives, tomatoes, and feta tapas in chile oil

Olives, tomatoes, and feta go perfectly with beer, making this one of my favorite tapas recipes. It makes more than you'll need for four people, but I find that the more glasses of beer I drink, the more I eat. Make extra and keep it in a covered bowl in the refrigerator to enjoy over several days—divine!

Remove the hard core from the tomatoes by making a V-shaped incision with a sharp knife. Put the tomatoes on the baking tray and sprinkle with salt and brown sugar. Push a slice of garlic into the soft seeds of each tomato, then roast in a preheated oven at 400°F for 1 hour until quite dry.

Put the tomatoes in a serving bowl, add the olives, cheese, chile oil, olive oil, and lemon zest. Toss well, top with the basil, then serve.

8 oz. vine-ripened tomatoes, halved

sea salt, to taste

brown sugar, to taste

2 garlic cloves, thinly sliced

1 cup green olives, about 5 oz.

1¼ cups black olives, about 8 oz., preferably Niçoise or Kalamata

8 oz. feta cheese, cut into cubes

2 tablespoons chile oil

2 tablespoons olive oil

grated zest of ½ unwaxed lemon

a handful of basil leaves

a baking tray

SERVES 4

smoky paprika-roasted potatoes

Smoked paprika transforms the humble baked potato into something special. Be restrained with the smoked paprika though—it is a very potent spice and should only be used in moderation.

1 teaspoon smoked paprika

4 teaspoons paprika

1 tablespoon olive oil, plus extra for sprinkling

1½ lb. fingerling potatoes

sea salt, to serve

SOUR CREAM TOPPING

a small handful of fresh dill, finely chopped

⅔ cup sour cream

1 garlic clove, crushed

freshly ground black pepper

a baking tray, lightly greased

SERVES 4

Put the prepared baking tray in a preheated oven at 400°F for 5 minutes.

Put the smoked and regular paprika in a bowl and mix. Put the olive oil in a second bowl, add the potatoes and turn until covered with oil. Roll each potato in the paprika mixture until evenly coated. Transfer to the hot baking tray and sprinkle with olive oil. Roast for 1 hour, or until the skins are golden and starting to crisp.

Meanwhile, to make the sour cream topping, put the dill, sour cream, garlic, and pepper in a bowl and mix well.

Cut a deep cross in each potato, then fill with the sour cream mixture. Sprinkle with salt and serve.

calabrian-style potatoes and peppers

This is a fine example of the "less is more" approach to entertaining—simple, good-quality ingredients cooked to perfection.

²/₃ cup olive oil

1 red bell pepper, halved, seeded, and thickly sliced

1 yellow bell pepper, halved, seeded, and thickly sliced

1¼ lb. Yukon gold potatoes, thinly sliced

sea salt and freshly ground black pepper

a small bunch of flat-leaf parsley, finely chopped, to serve (optional)

SERVES 4

Heat the oil in a large, lidded skillet. Add the red and yellow peppers and cook for 10 minutes, stirring occasionally, until starting to turn golden brown. Add the potatoes, salt, and pepper to the pan, cover with a lid, and cook for 5 minutes.

Remove the lid and continue cooking for 15 minutes, turning every few minutes as the potatoes begin to brown, taking care not to break them. If the potatoes start to stick, this will just add to the flavor of the dish, but don't let them burn.

When the potatoes are tender, transfer to a serving dish and top with the parsley, if using. Let cool for 5 minutes before serving.

beefsteak tomatoes

with garlic and herb butter

To be enjoyed at their absolute best, beefsteak tomatoes should be eaten hot and preferably in season. They make a great focal point for any meal and their lack of pretention is hugely appealing.

4 beefsteak tomatoes

3 garlic cloves, crushed

6 tablespoons unsalted butter, softened

1 teaspoon chile oil

a large handful of flat-leaf parsley, finely chopped

freshly ground black pepper

olive oil, for sprinkling

a baking tray

SERVES 4

Remove the stalk from each tomato and carefully cut out a small cavity for the filling.

Put the garlic, butter, chile oil, parsley, and pepper in a bowl and mix well. Fill the tomato cavities with the garlic mixture, pressing down gently as you go. Put on the baking tray, sprinkle with olive oil, and roast in a preheated oven at 300°F for 1 hour 20 minutes.

Eat hot from the oven with some of the cooking juices poured over the top.

green beans in tomato sauce

I really love the Italian tradition of bequeathing recipes to loved ones so that they can keep the heritage and spirit of the dish alive. This recipe and those on pages 38 and 45 have been passed unchanged down five generations. They have been very kindly shared by Gabi Matzeu, as enthusiastic an Italian chef as you will find. Good served hot or cold, this is stunning in its simplicity—no antipasti selection could be complete without it.

Put the olive and chile oils and garlic in a large saucepan and heat until the garlic has turned very lightly golden. Stir in the tomatoes, 1 cup water, and a large pinch of salt. Bring to a boil, then add the beans. Cover with a lid and cook gently for 30–40 minutes, stirring occasionally, until the beans are very tender.

COOK'S TIP

In Italy, it is a widely held belief that tomato seeds eaten in excess are bad for the liver. Thus, even simple canned tomatoes are passed through a mouli— a hand-operated rotary device—to remove the seeds. Moulis (food mills) are used extensively and are a classic kitchen utensil. They are superb for making purées, mashed vegetables, and removing the skin of legumes to make them more digestible.

¼ **cup olive oil**

1 **teaspoon chile oil**

1 **garlic clove, crushed**

4 **cups canned chopped tomatoes, two 16 oz. cans**

sea salt

1¼ **lb. green beans, stems removed**

SERVES 4

garlic mushrooms
in white wine and cream

One of the delights of cooking with mushrooms is that their flavor is so good you need add very few other ingredients. That said, the perfect partners for mushrooms are garlic and cream, a truly sublime combination.

Put the oil, butter, and garlic in a large saucepan and heat until the butter melts. Stir in the mushrooms and cook for 5–10 minutes until softened.

Add the wine and cream and bring to a boil. Reduce the heat slightly and continue cooking until the liquid has reduced by half. Season to taste, stir in the parsley, and serve.

COOK'S TIP

The best way to crush garlic is to slice it, add a pinch of salt, then crush it with a mortar and pestle. The salt draws out the juices to make a pulp.

1 tablespoon olive oil

4 tablespoons unsalted butter

3 garlic cloves, crushed

1 lb. cremini mushrooms, thickly sliced

½ cup white wine

¼ cup heavy cream

sea salt and freshly ground black pepper

a bunch of flat-leaf parsley, finely chopped

SERVES 4

1 large whole cauliflower, green leaves removed and reserved

2 onions, finely chopped

1¼ cups small green pitted olives, about 10 oz.

sea salt

⅓ cup olive oil, plus extra to serve

a small bunch of flat-leaf parsley, finely chopped, to serve

SERVES 4

sardinian cauliflower with olives

A spectacular way to serve a whole creamy head of cauliflower—let your guests serve themselves, pulling out the florets. There's no fuss needed for this gloriously simple dish.

Line a large, heavy saucepan with the reserved outer leaves from the cauliflower. Put the cauliflower on top. Sprinkle with the onion, olives, and some salt, then pour over the olive oil. Cover with a lid, set over the lowest heat, and cook gently for about 40 minutes or until tender—there should be no resistance when a fork is inserted into the middle of the cauliflower.

Carefully lift the cauliflower out of the saucepan and onto a large plate—be very careful not to break it. Pile the onion and olives on top, then sprinkle with the parsley and more olive oil and serve.

COOK'S TIP

Putting the outer leaves of the cauliflower in the bottom of the saucepan prevents the vegetable from burning or discoloring as it cooks—a great way to make use of something that would ordinarily be discarded.

BUFFETS

baby eggplant

with raisins and feta

Eggplant is used extensively in the Mediterranean, but no one cooks it quite like the Greeks. In this dish, the sweetness of the raisins and the saltiness of the feta act as the perfect balance to the acidity of the eggplant and tomatoes. Some people salt eggplant and leave it for 30 minutes before cooking to draw out the bitter juices, but I don't think this is necessary. If the vegetable is firm to the touch, just go ahead and use it with no messing about. If possible, make this dish the day before—it tastes even better if you give the flavors time to develop.

Put the olive oil, onion, and garlic in a large saucepan and sauté gently for 10 minutes until the onion is soft. Add the turmeric, cumin, coriander, garam masala, and paprika and continue to cook for a few more minutes. Stir in the tomatoes, sugar, pine nuts, and raisins, then transfer to a large ovenproof dish. Using a fork, prick the eggplant a few times so the juices can escape and absorb the flavor of the sauce. Add to the tomato sauce, then season with salt and pepper.

Cover the dish with foil and bake in a preheated oven at 400°F for 45 minutes. Remove the foil and continue cooking for a further 25 minutes. Let cool for 10 minutes, then sprinkle with the feta cheese and fresh mint and serve.

COOK'S TIP

The flavors of spices are intensified when lightly toasted. Sauté the spices in a dry skillet until they start to color and release their aroma. You can grind them with a mortar and pestle, but I prefer to use a coffee grinder (kept only for grinding spices), because it gives a finer texture. It is also much faster, which is especially important if you are cooking for large numbers!

2 tablespoons olive oil

1 onion, finely chopped

3 garlic cloves, crushed

1/2 teaspoon ground turmeric

2 teaspoons cumin seeds, lightly toasted in a dry skillet, then ground

1 tablespoon coriander seeds, lightly toasted in a dry skillet, then ground

1/2 teaspoon garam masala

1 teaspoon paprika

28 oz. canned chopped tomatoes

1 tablespoon brown sugar

1/2 cup pine nuts, toasted in a dry skillet until golden, about 1 1/2 oz.

1/3 cup raisins, about 2 oz.

1 lb. baby eggplant, left whole

sea salt and freshly ground black pepper

TO SERVE

4 oz. feta cheese, crumbled

chopped fresh mint

a large ovenproof dish

SERVES 6–8

roasted vegetable and ricotta loaf

This looks splendid displayed whole before being sliced. The cross-section looks good, too—a vision of colorful vegetables interwoven with creamy ricotta. It keeps well in the refrigerator for a couple of days.

Put the slices of eggplant on a baking tray, brush with olive oil, and sprinkle with salt and pepper. Preheat the oven to 400°F, then put the tray in the hottest part of the oven and roast for 20–25 minutes until the eggplant is tender. Put the red and yellow bell peppers and zucchini on the other baking tray, sprinkle with salt, and roast for about 20 minutes or until the peppers begin to blister and the zucchini are tender.

While all the vegetables are roasting, mix the ricotta with the lemon juice, garlic, parsley, chile, salt, and pepper.

When the eggplant are cooked, sprinkle with the vinegar. Put a damp cloth or plastic wrap over the bell peppers and set aside for 5–10 minutes (this makes the skins steam off and you can peel them more easily). Peel the peppers and cut each piece in half again.

Line the loaf pan with plastic wrap, then gently press slices of eggplant over the base and sides of the pan. Reserve 4 slices for the top. Spread generously with some of the ricotta mixture, then add a layer of yellow bell pepper, taking it up the sides of the pan if you can. Sprinkle with some of the basil, then spread with more ricotta mixture. Layer the red bell pepper next, followed by zucchini, adding a layer of the ricotta and basil after each vegetable. Top with the reserved eggplant slices. Cover the top with plastic wrap and put a weight on top. Leave overnight in the refrigerator.

Invert the loaf onto a plate and carefully pull away the plastic wrap. Using a serrated knife, cut into thick slices, then serve.

2 eggplant, cut lengthwise into about 5 slices

olive oil, for brushing

1 red bell pepper, halved and seeded

1 yellow bell pepper, halved and seeded

2 zucchini, sliced lengthwise

1 cup ricotta cheese, about 8 oz.

2 tablespoons lemon juice

1 garlic clove, crushed

a large handful of flat-leaf parsley, finely chopped

1 red chile, such as serrano, seeded and finely chopped

1 tablespoon balsamic vinegar

a large handful of basil leaves, torn

sea salt and freshly ground black pepper

2 large baking trays

a loaf pan, 2 lb.

SERVES 6–8

stuffed focaccia bread

Few things will make your guests feel more cared for than homemade bread. This superb focaccia really does not take too long to prepare, and the aroma is totally beguiling.

To make the dough, put the flour, salt, and yeast in a large bowl. Stir in the olive oil and 1½ cups water, then bring the dough together with your hands. Knead the dough by hand until it is smooth and springy to the touch (this should take about 10 minutes) or knead in a machine with a dough hook attachment. Return to the bowl and lightly oil the top to prevent it from drying out. Cover with plastic wrap or a damp dish towel and let rise in a warm place for 30 minutes until doubled in size.

Meanwhile, to prepare the filling, put the bell peppers and onion in a roasting pan, sprinkle with olive oil and salt, and roast in a preheated oven at 350°F for 15 minutes. Remove from the oven and let cool. Transfer to a bowl, add the mozzarella, basil, tomatoes, oil, olives, salt, and pepper, and mix well.

When the dough has risen to double its original size, transfer to a lightly floured surface and cut in half. Roll out the first half to the size of the baking tray and use to line the tray. Spread the filling over the top, leaving a 1-inch border around the edge. Roll out the remaining dough and put on top of the filling. Press the edges of the dough together to seal.

Brush with the 2 teaspoons olive oil, sprinkle with salt, and dot with sprigs of rosemary, then let rise for a further 30 minutes. Just before cooking, use your thumb to make lots of indentations in the dough—this looks very attractive when cooked. Bake in a preheated oven at 350°F for 40 minutes until lightly golden.

COOK'S TIP

Try to time your cooking so that your guests are greeted by the aroma of freshly baked bread—there will much excitement all round.

3⅓ cups white bread flour

1 teaspoon sea salt

¼ oz. package active dry yeast

1 tablespoon olive oil

FILLING

½ red bell pepper, halved, seeded, and sliced

½ orange bell pepper, halved, seeded, and sliced

1 red onion, sliced

olive oil, for roasting

8 oz. mozzarella cheese, cut into cubes

a large handful of fresh basil, chopped

8 sun-dried tomatoes in oil, sliced

1 tablespoon oil from the jar of tomatoes

a handful of pitted black olives

sea salt and freshly ground black pepper

TO FINISH

2 teaspoons extra virgin olive oil

sea salt

small sprigs of rosemary

a baking tray, lightly greased and floured

SERVES 6–8

spinach and blue cheese phyllo pastries

with apricots and pine nuts

These pastries offer a lovely array of tastes and textures the spinach provides a neutral backdrop for the rich cheese, sweet fruit, and crunchy pine nuts, all wrapped up in a crisp phyllo shell. They make quite a sensation—and they also freeze superbly.

1 tablespoon olive oil

12 oz. spinach, washed well

1/2 teaspoon ground nutmeg

1 garlic clove, crushed

a small handful of fresh dill, coarsely chopped

6 oz. blue cheese, such as dolcelatte, cut into small cubes

2 oz. dried apricots, about 3–4, soaked overnight, drained, and sliced

1/2 cup pine nuts, toasted in a dry skillet until golden, about 2 oz.

8 oz. phyllo pastry dough (1/2 package)

olive oil or melted butter, for brushing

crisp salad leaves, to serve (optional)

sea salt and freshly ground black pepper

a baking tray, lightly oiled

MAKES 6 ROLLS

Heat the oil in a wok or skillet over medium heat. Add the spinach, nutmeg, and garlic and stir-fry until the spinach has just wilted. Drain through a colander and let cool, then squeeze out the liquid with the back of a spoon. Put the spinach mixture in a bowl and add the dill, blue cheese, apricots, pine nuts, and salt and pepper to taste.

Cut 2 sheets of the phyllo dough to about 12 x 6 inches. Put 1 sheet on a work surface and brush with oil or melted butter. Put the second sheet on top. Divide the filling into 6 portions. Spoon 1 portion along the narrow edge and firmly roll up the double layer of dough, tucking in the ends as you go. Repeat until all the filling has been used and you have 6 rolls.

Transfer to the prepared baking tray and bake in a preheated oven at 350°F for 25 minutes, then turn over and cook for a further 15 minutes. Serve 1 roll per person, with a few crisp salad leaves, if using.

trottole pasta with bell peppers and garlic

I try to avoid using pasta because it seems to have become so synonymous with vegetarian dining. However, for a buffet I think pasta is a great idea—it really does appeal to everybody. This recipe lends itself to a large occasion because the vegetables and bread can be prepared in advance, then left overnight to soak up the flavors of the olive oil, garlic, and vinegar. As the guests are due, toss in the pasta, basil, salt, and pepper.

Put the tomato, peppers, bread, and garlic in a large bowl with the olive oil and vinegar. Leave for a couple of hours or overnight to develop the flavors.

Cook the pasta according to the instructions on the package. Drain and cool under cold running water. Drain again, then mix the pasta and basil into the vegetables. Add salt and pepper to taste and serve.

1 beefsteak tomato, cut into tiny cubes

1/2 red bell pepper, halved, seeded, then cut into tiny squares

1/2 yellow bell pepper, halved, seeded, then cut into tiny squares

1/2 orange bell pepper, halved, seeded, then cut into tiny squares

4 oz. ciabatta bread, cut into tiny pieces (stale bread also works well)

2 garlic cloves, crushed

3/4 cup good quality extra virgin olive oil

2 tablespoons balsamic vinegar

16 oz. spiral pasta, such as trottole or fusilli

a large bunch of basil leaves, coarsely chopped

sea salt and freshly ground black pepper

SERVES 6–8

nectarine and raspberry tart

with vanilla cream

This is a sumptuous-looking dessert that isn't too calorific! For a variation on the theme, try using peaches, blueberries, and blackberries with red currants sprinkled over the top.

To make the vanilla cream, put the milk and vanilla bean in a medium saucepan, bring to a boil, then remove from the heat.

Put the egg yolks, sugar, and cornstarch in a separate bowl. Using electric beaters, beat until pale and creamy, then mix in the hot milk. Reduce the heat to low, then return the mixture to the pan, stirring constantly until it has thickened. Remove the vanilla bean, then stir in the melted butter. Transfer to a bowl, cover with plastic wrap or wax paper to prevent a skin from forming, then let cool.

To make the tart, roll out the dough and use it to line the baking tray. Pour the vanilla cream over the top leaving a 1-inch border around the edge. Arrange alternate slices of nectarines and plums on top of the cream. Brush the exposed dough with melted butter. Sprinkle the brown sugar over the fruit and cook in a preheated oven at 400°F for 25 minutes until golden.

Serve with the fresh raspberries sprinkled over the top and a dusting of confectioners' sugar.

COOK'S TIP

To make vanilla sugar, break a couple of vanilla beans in half and put in a jar with a lid. Pour the sugar on top. Leave for 1 day before using, and keep refilling with more sugar. When you remove the lid, you're assailed with a divine vanilla fragrance.

VANILLA CREAM

1½ cups milk

1 vanilla bean, split in half lengthwise

4 egg yolks

⅓ cup vanilla sugar or sugar

2 tablespoons cornstarch

2 tablespoons unsalted butter, melted

FRUIT TART

13 oz. puff pastry dough

3 nectarines, thinly sliced

3 plums, sliced (yellow plums look very pretty)

melted butter, for brushing

½ tablespoon brown sugar

6 oz. raspberries, about ½ dry pint

confectioners' sugar, for dusting

a baking tray, about 9 x 12 inches

SERVES 6–8

SPONGE CAKE

1 stick unsalted butter, softened

1 cup plus 1 tablespoon sugar

4 large eggs, lightly beaten

1/3 cup all-purpose flour

3 cups ground almonds*

MINT SYRUP

3 tablespoons sugar

12 mint leaves, finely chopped

TRIFLE FILLING

1 lb. mascarpone cheese

2 tablespoons sugar

3 egg yolks

8 oz. raspberries, about 3/4 dry pint

8 oz. strawberries

a small handful of fresh mint leaves

a cake pan, 8-inches diameter, lined with wax paper

SERVES 6

*If your supermarket doesn't have ground almonds, use 10 oz. slivered almonds and grind them in a food processor or with a mortar and pestle.

strawberry and mascarpone trifle

This extraordinarily versatile dessert is perfect for a warm, lazy day. Red fruit always looks magnificent but you could also use blueberries, mangoes, and passionfruit. Only about half of the sponge is necessary for this trifle, so freeze the rest for an extra-speedy version next time round. The sponge has a dense, chewy texture to absorb the mint syrup. The mint is a perfect partner for the strawberries, but you could also use fruit juice or sweet wine.

To make the sponge cake, put the butter and sugar in a medium bowl and beat with electric beaters until the mixture is pale and creamy. Slowly add the eggs, beating well between each addition. Using a metal spoon, fold in the flour and ground almonds.

Spoon the mixture into the prepared cake pan and bake in the center of a preheated oven at 350°F for 40 minutes until springy to the touch or until a skewer can be removed cleanly when inserted into the middle.

To make the mint syrup, put the sugar, mint and 1/3 cup water in a small saucepan. Bring to a boil and continue to boil until reduced by one-third.

To make the filling, put the mascarpone, sugar and egg yolks in a bowl. Using electric beaters, beat the mixture until creamy. Using a fork, lightly mash the raspberries to a purée. Chop half the strawberries into small pieces, and cut the remainder in half, leaving the stems intact for decoration.

To assemble the trifle, break the cake into large pieces and put into a large dish or 6 individual dishes. Moisten the cake with the mint syrup and add some of the mint leaves. Spoon in the raspberry purée, then the chopped strawberries, then the mascarpone. Top with the strawberry halves, then chill in the refrigerator for at least 1 hour before serving.

CASUAL LUNCHES

buckwheat noodles in miso ginger broth

This dish is a meal in itself and incredibly versatile. Mushrooms, snow peas, broccoli, baby corn, or Chinese leaf all work well—use whatever is in season, or more to the point, what's in the refrigerator! The same applies to the noodles. I like buckwheat noodles because they thicken the dish slightly and have a wonderful nutty flavor. Use your favorite—the choice is endless with both fresh and dried noodles.

Cook the noodles according to the package instructions, then rinse well.

Put the sesame and safflower oils, onion, chile, ginger, and soy sauce in a large saucepan. Cook gently for 10 minutes until the onion is soft, then stir in the stock and beans. Bring gently to a boil, then add the carrots and oyster mushrooms. Continue cooking for 2–3 minutes, then add the bok choy and cooked noodles. Again, continue simmering for 1–2 minutes. Add the miso, enoki mushrooms, bean sprouts, and scallions, then serve immediately while the vegetables are still crunchy and vibrant in color.

COOK'S TIPS

Miso is a fermented paste of soybeans. There are various types depending on the culture used to ferment the beans—barley, rice, and wheat are all available. The miso is stirred in at the end of the cooking process so that its nutritional content is not diminished.

Enoki mushrooms are small mushrooms with long stems and tiny white caps. They are usually bought in clumps with the root base still attached—this is removed before cooking.

If you are using fresh noodles, there is no need to precook them. Simply stir them in with the bok choy.

6 oz. dried buckwheat noodles

1 teaspoon toasted sesame oil

1 tablespoon safflower oil

1 red onion, finely chopped

1 red chile, seeded and finely chopped

1 inch fresh ginger, peeled and grated

¼ cup soy sauce

1 quart vegetable stock

6 oz. green beans, topped

6 oz. carrots, cut into matchsticks

4 oz. oyster mushrooms, thickly sliced, about 2 cups

8 oz. bok choy, cut into thick rounds

3 tablespoons miso paste

4 oz. enoki mushrooms, root base removed

6 oz. bean sprouts, rinsed and drained, about 1½ cups

7 scallions, cut lengthwise into strips

SERVES 4

POLENTA (CORNMEAL) ROUNDS

5 tablespoons unsalted butter

1 tablespoon olive oil

1 garlic clove, crushed

4 cups vegetable stock

1 cup polenta or yellow cornmeal

8 scallions, thinly sliced

4 oz. spinach, thinly sliced, about 1 cup

sea salt and freshly ground black pepper

8 oz. mozzarella cheese, sliced

ROASTED VEGETABLES

1½ lb. butternut squash, peeled, cut in half, with seeds removed

1 red Cubanelle pepper, halved and seeded, or regular bell pepper

1 yellow Cubanelle pepper, halved and seeded, or regular bell pepper

2 red onions, cut into wedges

1 whole head of garlic, cloves separated but skins left on

4 heads of baby fennel, quartered, or 2 medium heads of fennel, thickly sliced

a handful of thyme sprigs, stalks left on

a handful of oregano sprigs, stalks left on

2 sprigs of fresh rosemary

¼ cup olive oil

8 oz. cherry tomatoes

15 asparagus spears

¼ cup balsamic vinegar

sea salt and freshly ground black pepper

2 large baking trays, 14 x 9 inches

a cookie cutter, 3-inches diameter

SERVES 4

spinach and mozzarella polenta
with roasted vegetables, herbs, and balsamic

Roasting must be one of the simplest of all cooking techniques. It reinforces the idea that when good-quality ingredients are used, very little has to be done to them. It brings out the natural sweetness of the vegetables and here this is complemented by the contrasting, oaky flavor of balsamic vinegar. Include as many different-colored vegetables as possible, cut them into different shapes and don't be tempted to cook everything at once.

To make the polenta, put the butter, oil, and garlic in a medium saucepan. Cook lightly, then add the stock and bring to a boil. Pour in the polenta, beating constantly, then add the scallions and spinach. Add salt and pepper to taste, then continue stirring. Cook as instructed on the polenta package—the time will vary depending on the type of polenta used. Spoon into one of the baking trays and set side for about 2 hours, or until firm to the touch.

To cook the vegetables, put all the vegetables, except the tomatoes and asparagus, on the second baking tray. Sprinkle with the herbs, olive oil, salt, and pepper and mix well. Roast in a preheated oven at 400°F for 30 minutes, then stir in the tomatoes and asparagus. Continue cooking for a further 20 minutes until all the vegetables are tender.

Invert the polenta onto a work surface and cut out 8 rounds with the cookie cutter. Brush the baking tray with olive oil and arrange the rounds on the tray. Top each round with a slice of mozzarella and bake in the oven for 10–15 minutes.

Put 2 rounds of polenta on each plate, add the roasted vegetables, then sprinkle with 1 tablespoon balsamic vinegar. Serve immediately.

VARIATION

Try this with roasted chunks of eggplant, carrots, zucchini, patty pan squash, or sweet potatoes.

gado gado salad
with hot satay sauce

This is a dish full of contrasts: a rich, hot, and spicy sauce served over a cool, crunchy, fragrant salad. Fantastically healthy and well balanced, too. The sauce also freezes excellently—make extra and keep the rest for another day.

Put the potatoes in a saucepan, add a pinch of salt and water to cover, bring to a boil, and simmer for 15 minutes, or until tender. Drain, let cool, cut into thick slices and transfer to a large serving bowl.

Bring another saucepan of salted water to a boil and plunge in the beans. Cook for 5 minutes until tender. Remove and cool under cold running water. Drain and add to the bowl. Using the same water, cook the carrots for 3–4 minutes until tender but retaining a little bite. Remove and cool under cold running water. Drain and add to the bowl.

Stir in the cabbage, cucumber, bean sprouts, and cilantro.

Meanwhile, pour the sesame oil into a skillet and heat gently. Stir in the eggs and cook for 2–3 minutes until just set. Invert the omelet onto a plate, then flip back into the pan to cook the other side for a further 2–3 minutes. Transfer to a chopping board, roll up into a cylinder, then let cool. Cut into slices when cool.

Put the peanuts on the baking tray and roast in a preheated oven at 400°F for about 15 minutes or until starting to color. Toss with the soy sauce and return to the oven for a further 5 minutes. Crush the nuts in a food processor, or by wrapping them in a dish towel and crushing with a rolling pin. Stir the nuts and omelet strips into the salad, then add salt and pepper to taste.

To make the satay sauce, put the safflower and sesame oils, onion, chile, garlic, and ginger in a saucepan and cook gently for 10 minutes until the onion is very soft. Stir in the coconut milk, tomato ketchup, peanut butter, soy sauce, lime juice, and salt and continue cooking for a further 10 minutes. Transfer to a food processor and blend until completely smooth.

Serve the salad piled high on a plate with the hot sauce poured over the top.

COOK'S TIP

This sauce is very good stirred through noodles, then topped with cilantro and sesame seeds. Quick and delicious.

14 oz. fingerling potatoes

6 oz. green beans, stems removed

8 oz. carrots, cut into long matchsticks

10 oz. white cabbage, cored and thinly sliced, 3 cups

6 oz. cucumber, cut lengthwise into quarters, then sliced into chunky pieces, about 2 cups

1½ cups bean sprouts, about 6 oz., rinsed and drained

a big handful of cilantro, coarsely chopped

1 teaspoon toasted sesame oil

4 eggs, lightly beaten

1 cup raw unsalted peanuts, about 6 oz.

1 tablespoon soy sauce

sea salt and freshly ground black pepper

SATAY SAUCE

1 tablespoon safflower oil

1 teaspoon toasted sesame oil

1 red onion, finely chopped

1–2 red chiles, finely chopped

2 garlic cloves, crushed

1 inch fresh ginger, peeled and grated

1¾ cups canned coconut milk

2 tablespoons tomato ketchup

3 tablespoons organic peanut butter

1 tablespoon soy sauce

freshly squeezed juice of 1 lime

sea salt

a baking tray

SERVES 4

roasted butternut squash risotto

Butternut squash is up there as one of my all-time favorite vegetables. It's wonderful—the best of the huge range of squashes available, with a lovely deep orange hue. Roasting heightens its sweetness, and with cream, butter, or cheese makes for a fantastic harmony of flavors.

Put the squash on a baking tray and sprinkle with salt and 2 tablespoons olive oil. Roast in a preheated oven at 400°F for 30 minutes until tender.

Put the butter, remaining 2 tablespoons olive oil, and garlic in a medium saucepan. Cook gently for 2 minutes, then add the oregano, sage, and rice. Let the rice absorb the buttery juices, then stir in a ladle of the hot stock. Wait until the stock has been absorbed, then add the wine and the rest of the stock, a ladle at a time, making sure it has been completely absorbed between each addition. Stir in the squash and lightly mash with the back of a fork, leaving some pieces whole. Stir in the lemon juice and add salt and pepper to taste.

Serve topped with a generous spoonful of mascarpone.

COOK'S TIP

The risotto is good served with a light salad of lamb's lettuce (mâche), thin slices of roasted zucchini, and cherry tomatoes or steamed vegetables.

1 butternut squash (about 2 lb.), peeled, seeded, and cut into small cubes

¼ cup olive oil

4 tablespoons unsalted butter

2 garlic cloves, crushed

a handful of fresh oregano leaves, finely chopped

10 sage leaves

1¼ cups risotto rice, such as arborio

5 cups hot vegetable stock

¾ cup white wine

1 teaspoon lemon juice

sea salt and freshly ground black pepper

mascarpone cheese, to serve

a baking tray

SERVES 4

leek, feta, and black olive tart

with endive and watercress salad

This tart can be made with a multitude of complementary toppings: onion, thyme, and blue cheese; wild mushroom and goat cheese; or spinach, ricotta, and pine nuts. It is quite substantial, so take advantage of the vast array of leaves now available and serve with a tasty but light salad. I like to use the slightly bitter salad leaves because they cut through the richness of the tart very well.

LEEK TART

13 oz. puff pastry dough (from 17 oz. box), thawed if frozen

1 tablespoon olive oil

14 oz. leeks, thinly sliced, about 2¼ cups

a large handful of fresh dill, coarsely chopped

8 oz. feta cheese, cut into small cubes

4 oz. pitted black olives, about ⅔ cup

sea salt

a baking pan, about 12 x 8 inches

a baking tray

SERVES 4–6

Roll out the dough to fit the pan almost exactly. Trim and discard a tiny strip around the edge of the dough so that it will rise evenly.

Heat a wok or skillet, add the oil and leeks, and stir-fry. Add just a little salt, then stir in the dill. Transfer to a colander to drain. Let cool.

Arrange the leeks over the dough. Top with the feta and olives. Bake in a preheated oven at 400°F for 35 minutes, or until the crust has risen and is golden brown.

Serve with the endive salad (right).

ENDIVE AND WATERCRESS SALAD

1 cup walnuts, about 4 oz.

1 tablespoon soy sauce

1 teaspoon chile oil

2 heads of Belgian endive, halved lengthwise

freshly squeezed juice of ½ lime

6 oz. watercress

1 small head of radicchio, cored and shredded

1 oz. dried mango, soaked overnight, then sliced into long strips

DRESSING

⅔ cup sour cream

1 tablespoon lemon juice

2 teaspoons truffle oil (optional)

1 garlic clove, crushed

salt and freshly ground black pepper

a baking tray

SERVES 4–6

Put the walnuts on the baking tray and roast in the center of a preheated oven at 400°F for 15 minutes, or until golden and aromatic. Sprinkle with soy sauce and chile oil, toss well, then return to the oven for a further 10 minutes. Let cool.

Cut the endive into long strips and put in a large salad bowl. Add the lime juice and toss to prevent discoloration. Add the walnuts, watercress, radicchio, and mango strips.

Mix the dressing ingredients in a small bowl and serve separately so that the colors of the salad won't be masked by the sour cream.

exotic fruit scrunch

There are no limits to this dessert, which can be made with any fruits you like. The top can be decorated as extravagantly as you dare using grated or melted chocolate, lightly toasted unsweetened flaked coconut or flaked almonds, or a purée of strained raspberries sprinkled "Jackson-Pollock-style" over the top! For anyone who feels guilty about desserts, take heart—the topping includes nearly as much yogurt as cream.

Put the flour and oats in a medium bowl and mix well. Using your fingertips, rub in the butter until the mixture resembles bread crumbs. Stir in the brown sugar, then press the mixture firmly onto the prepared tray. Bake in a preheated oven at 400°F for 15 minutes until lightly golden. Let cool, then break it up into large random pieces.

To make the cream topping, whip the cream until soft peaks form. Stir in the yogurt and confectioners' sugar to taste.

Put the pieces of oat scrunch in a large glass serving bowl or individual glasses, top with the papaya and mango, then the cream and yogurt mixture and the figs. Scoop the passionfruit flesh and seeds over the top and serve.

CRISPY OAT SCRUNCH

$1/2$ cup all-purpose or whole wheat flour

1 cup whole rolled oats

4 tablespoons unsalted butter

$1/4$ cup brown sugar

CREAM TOPPING

$1 1/4$ cups heavy cream

$3/4$ cup plain yogurt

$1/3$ cup confectioners' sugar, or to taste

EXOTIC FRUIT LAYERS

2 medium papayas (about 1 lb.), peeled, seeded, and sliced

$1 1/4$ lb. mangoes, peeled, seeded, and sliced (about 1 large)

2 figs, quartered

4 passionfruit, halved

a baking tray, 12 x 8 inches, oiled

SERVES 4

6 tablespoons unsalted butter, softened

1 cup sugar

3 eggs, separated

1 teaspoon vanilla extract

3⅓ cups cream cheese, about 1½ lb., softened

2 teaspoons cornstarch

1 teaspoon baking powder

TO SERVE

a selection of summer berries, such as raspberries, red currants, and blueberries

confectioners' sugar, for dusting

a jelly roll pan, 12 x 8 inches, greased and lined with parchment paper

SERVES 6

polish cheesecake
with summer berries

This rich, dense, but surprisingly light cheesecake is served in shallow slices. It works equally well served with a strong espresso or as a dessert at the end of a meal. Try it with summer berries, as here, or with rhubarb purée.

Put the butter, sugar, egg yolks, and vanilla extract in a bowl. Beat with electric beaters until the mixture is pale and creamy.

Put the egg whites in a clean, dry bowl and beat until soft peaks form.

Using a metal spoon, very lightly stir the cream cheese, cornstarch, and baking powder into the butter mixture. Add the egg whites and mix lightly.

Spoon into the prepared jelly roll pan and spread evenly with a spatula. Bake in a preheated oven at 300° for 1 hour. Remove from the oven and let cool in the pan—the cake will flatten naturally.

Cut the cheesecake into 12 portions and gently ease away from the parchment paper. Very carefully remove the slices of cheesecake, taking care not to break them. Put 2 slices on each plate, top with the berries, dust with confectioners' sugar, then serve.

FORMAL DINNERS

moroccan tagine with harissa

The two main ingredients in a tagine are usually meat and dried fruit. This vegetarian twist uses chickpeas as the protein element. It works equally well, especially when served with spicy harissa sauce and crispy couscous fritters. Harissa sauce is widely available in French or North African gourmet stores if you haven't the time to make your own.

CHICKPEA TAGINE

2 tablespoons olive oil

1/2 red onion, thinly sliced

1/2 white onion, thinly sliced

1 teaspoon ground turmeric

2 teaspoons cumin seeds

2 teaspoons coriander seeds, lightly toasted in a dry skillet and ground

1 teaspoon ground cinnamon

1 red serrano chile, seeded and finely chopped

3 cups canned chopped tomatoes, about 28 oz.

1 tablespoon tomato paste

2 oz. dried apricots, soaked overnight, drained and sliced

1/4 cup raisins, soaked overnight, about 1 oz.

1/2 cup black olives, such as Niçoise or Kalamata, pitted, about 3 oz.

1 large baking potato, cut into wedges

8 oz. carrots, thickly sliced, about 2 cups

1/2 small green cabbage, cored and thinly sliced

2 1/2 cups chickpeas, about 1 lb., soaked overnight, drained, and cooked for 1–1 1/2 hours until tender

a large bunch of flat-leaf parsley, finely chopped

a large bunch of cilantro, finely chopped

sea salt and freshly ground black pepper

SERVES 4

HARISSA SAUCE

3 large fresh red chiles

1 garlic clove

2 teaspoons coriander seeds, lightly toasted in a dry skillet and ground

1 teaspoon cumin seeds, lightly roasted in a dry skillet and ground

1/4 cup olive oil

1 teaspoon tomato paste

a pinch of salt

Put the chiles in a dry skillet and cook over gentle heat, until the skins begin to blacken and blister. Remove from the heat, let cool, then remove the seeds.

Put the chiles, garlic, coriander, cumin, olive oil, tomato paste, and salt in a blender and process until smooth. Use to taste in this recipe, then keep the remainder for another occasion. (It will keep, sealed, in the refrigerator for 2–3 weeks.)

Heat half the oil in a large saucepan. Add the red and white onions, turmeric, cumin, coriander, cinnamon, and chile and cook gently for 10 minutes until the onions are softened and translucent. Stir in the tomatoes and tomato paste and cook for 10 minutes. Add the apricots, raisins, olives, potato, and carrots. Continue cooking slowly for about 45 minutes, until the carrots are tender.

Heat the remaining oil in a wok or skillet, add the cabbage, and stir-fry until just starting to soften. Add to the saucepan, then add the cooked chickpeas and bring to a boil. Stir in the parsley and cilantro and season with salt and pepper to taste.

couscous fritters

1/3 cup couscous, about 4 oz.

a bunch of flat-leaf parsley, finely chopped

a small handful of fresh mint leaves, finely chopped

4 oz. feta cheese, cut into small cubes

1 teaspoon cumin seeds

1 teaspoon coriander seeds, lightly toasted in a dry skillet and ground

1/2 teaspoon ground turmeric

2 tablespoons lemon juice

1 tablespoon olive oil

2 eggs, 1 lightly beaten

1/4 cup all-purpose flour, plus extra to coat

sea salt and freshly ground black pepper

4 cups bread crumbs, made with stale white bread

safflower oil, for sautéing

MAKES 12–14

Put the couscous in a bowl and cover with 1 cup cold water. Let soak for 10 minutes, then fluff it up with a fork. Stir in the parsley, mint, feta, cumin, coriander, turmeric, lemon juice, olive oil, the whole egg, and salt and pepper. Mix well, then stir in the flour. Shape into 12–14 balls and press slightly flat.

Put the beaten egg, extra flour, and bread crumbs onto 3 separate plates. Dip the balls first in the egg, then the flour, then the bread crumbs. Pour 1/2 inch oil into a skillet and heat until a cube of bread will turn golden in 1 minute. Add the fritters in small batches, spacing them well apart in the pan, and cook for 3–4 minutes until golden on both sides. Drain on paper towels and keep them warm in a low oven while you cook the remainder.

Serve the fritters next to the tagine with harissa sauce sprinkled over the top.

COOK'S TIP

Chiles respond very well to roasting. I like to dry-roast them in a skillet on top of the oven so that I can keep an eye on them. If chiles burn, the whole room will fill with a hot, spicy, choking aroma that takes an age to dissipate—not to be recommended!

8 oz. phyllo pastry dough
(½ package)

2½ tablespoons butter,
melted

PACKAGE FILLING

10 oz. tomatoes
(about 3 small)

1 tablespoon olive oil

1 teaspoon coriander
seeds

1 teaspoon cumin seeds

1 garlic clove, crushed

½ red chile, seeded and
finely chopped

1 cup couscous

⅓ cup dried chickpeas,
soaked in water
overnight, drained, and
cooked for 1–1½ hours

3 oz. dried apricots,
soaked in water overnight,
drained, and sliced

⅓ cup raisins, soaked in
water overnight

¾ cup slivered almonds,
lightly toasted in a dry
skillet

a handful of flat-leaf
parsley, finely chopped

a handful of fresh mint
leaves, finely chopped

7 oz. feta cheese, cubed

freshly squeezed juice of
1 lemon

sea salt and freshly
ground black pepper

feta and chickpea packages
with onion and tomato chutney

For these savory pastries, I leave the spices whole so that the full experience can be enjoyed. Coupled with couscous, they give it the lift it needs. Some people are surprised by the use of fruit in a savory dish, but it is very typical of Middle Eastern cuisine. The sweetness of the dried fruit cuts through the saltiness of the cheese and diffuses the heat from any chile. These pastries are delicious eaten hot or cold as part of a picnic. They can also be made much smaller and served as fingerfood. Usually, I serve them with spinach wilted with a pinch of nutmeg and the grated zest of 2 lemons, together with a bowl of yogurt spiced with chile, turmeric, coriander, and cumin, all toasted. Delicious.

RED ONION, TOMATO,
AND OLIVE CHUTNEY

1 red onion, finely
chopped

1 lb. tomatoes (about
4 small), quartered

1 tablespoon olive oil

½ cup pitted black olives,
finely chopped

sea salt and freshly
ground black pepper

2 baking trays

SERVES 4

To make the filling for the packages, mix the tomatoes with the olive oil, spices, garlic, and chile. Season with salt, then transfer to a baking tray. Roast in a preheated oven at 400°F for 20 minutes until they collapse in on themselves.

Meanwhile, put the couscous in a bowl, add 1¾ cups cold water, and let soak for 10 minutes. Fluff up with a fork, then transfer to a large bowl with the chickpeas, apricots, raisins, almonds, herbs, feta, lemon juice, salt, and pepper. Stir in the roasted tomatoes and mix well.

To prepare the chutney, put the red onion and tomatoes on a baking tray, sprinkle with olive oil, then roast at 400°F for 20 minutes until tender. Transfer to a bowl and stir in the olives, mixing thoroughly. Add salt and pepper to taste.

Reduce the oven to 350°F. Put 3 sheets of the phyllo dough on a work surface, overlaying them so that they form a star shape, and brush each sheet lightly with the melted butter. (Keep the rest of the phyllo covered with a damp cloth to prevent it drying out.)

Divide the filling into 4 portions and put 1 portion in the middle of the top sheet of phyllo, then pull up all the sides, twisting and pinching so that the filling is encased and the dough is sealed. Repeat to make 4 generously sized packages. Bake for 20 minutes until lightly golden, then cover with foil and cook for a further 15 minutes.

Serve the phyllo packages with the chutney on the side, and perhaps some wilted lemon spinach and spicy yogurt (see recipe introduction).

mushrooms in ale and cream

with parsnip rösti and white bean mash

This dish is guaranteed to render guests speechless with anticipation and admiration. Mushrooms are often used in vegetarian cookery—and with good reason. Their distinctive flavor and heady aroma are very appealing and, with wild mushrooms, a truly exotic dish can be created. You can use the traditional potato for the rösti if you prefer, although I like the sweetness of parsnips. Coupled with the mellow bean mash, all the flavors are easy to decipher and enjoy. Serve with steamed broccoli for a flash of color.

3 tablespoons unsalted butter

1 tablespoon olive oil

4 oz. shiitake mushrooms, sliced

8 oz. cremini mushrooms, sliced

4 oz. wild mushrooms, sliced

4 oz. portobello mushrooms, sliced

4 garlic cloves, crushed

1 teaspoon paprika

1/2 cup dark ale

3/4 cup heavy cream

1 tablespoon lemon juice

sea salt and freshly ground black pepper

fresh dill, coarsely chopped, to serve

WHITE BEAN MASH

8 oz. baking potatoes, cut into chunks

1 1/4 cups dried white beans, about 7 oz., soaked overnight, drained, and cooked for 1 hour (reserving 5 tablespoons of the cooking liquid)

2 garlic cloves, chopped

freshly squeezed juice of 1/2 lemon

1/2 cup olive oil

PARSNIP RÖSTI

1 1/2 lb. parsnips, grated

1/2 teaspoon ground nutmeg

2 egg yolks, lightly beaten

2 tablespoons all-purpose flour

6 tablespoons unsalted butter

1/4 cup safflower oil

sea salt and freshly ground pepper

a skillet, 6-inches diameter

SERVES 4

To make the bean mash, cook the potatoes in a large saucepan of boiling salted water for 15 minutes or until tender. Drain and keep them warm. Put the drained beans in a food processor with the potatoes and garlic. Mix the reserved bean cooking liquid, lemon juice, and olive oil in a small pitcher, then, with the machine running, pour into the processor in a steady stream. Transfer the mash to a bowl and keep it warm.

To prepare the mushrooms, melt the butter and olive oil in a large skillet. Add the 4 kinds of mushrooms, garlic, and paprika, and sauté gently for 5 minutes until they start to soften. Stir in the ale and cream. Continue to cook for about 10–15 minutes until the liquid has reduced by half. Stir in the lemon juice and add salt and pepper to taste.

To make the rösti, put the grated parsnips in a colander and squeeze out any surplus juices with your hands. Put the parsnips in a bowl and stir in the nutmeg, egg yolks, flour, salt, and pepper. Melt 1 1/2 tablespoons of the butter with 1 tablespoon of the oil in the skillet. Divide the parsnips mixture in 4 and press 1 portion into the skillet, pushing down firmly with a wooden spoon. Cook for 4–5 minutes over medium heat until golden brown and crispy. Invert onto a plate, slide back into the pan, and cook the other side for a further 4–5 minutes. Don't worry if the rösti breaks up slightly—just mold it back together with the spoon. Repeat to make another 3 rösti.

To serve, spoon a generous mound of mashed bean mixture on 4 plates, then flatten slightly. Top with a rösti, making sure a little of the mash is visible around the edges. Add the mushrooms so that they are nestled on top of the rösti. Top with dill and serve.

COOK'S TIP

Mushrooms are like sponges and soak up flavorings very easily. But if they are washed they become waterlogged and lose the capacity to absorb anything else. Therefore, always wipe mushrooms with a damp cloth before cooking, rather than rinsing them.

1½ lb. deep-fried tofu, cut into chunks

2 tablespoons soy sauce

½ teaspoon chile oil

2 tablespoons safflower oil

1 tablespoon sesame oil

10 oz. carrots, cut into matchsticks

8 oz. shiitake mushrooms, thickly sliced

2 tablespoons hoisin sauce

1 tablespoon rice vinegar

9 scallions, cut into 1-inch strips

sea salt and freshly ground black pepper

RICE PATTIES

1 cup uncooked black rice (not wild rice)

1 tablespoon soy sauce

1 teaspoon sweet chile sauce

1 egg yolk

3 heaping tablespoons all-purpose flour

a handful of fresh chives, thinly sliced

a handful of cilantro, finely chopped

sea salt and freshly ground black pepper

safflower oil, for sautéing

TO FINISH

1 large bok choy, thickly sliced

coarsely chopped cilantro, to serve

a baking tray

SERVES 4

tofu and shiitake mushrooms
on crispy black rice patties

Rice is a staple food in the East, but in the West we have probably been a little slow in recognizing its health benefits and have also been limited by meager choice. However, stores now offer a huge range of rice, including black, red, scented, and sticky varieties. The black rice used for these patties is wonderful and lends an unusual color to the dish.

To make the patties, put the rice and soy sauce in a saucepan and cook according to the instructions on the package. When cooked, drain through a colander and rinse until the water runs clear. Put the rice in a bowl and mash with the chile sauce, egg yolk, flour, chives, cilantro, salt, and pepper. Roll into 12 balls and flatten into patties. Heat about 1 inch depth oil in a wok. When the oil is hot, drop in the patties a few at a time, and cook for a few minutes on each side until crisp and golden. Drain on paper towels and keep them warm.

Put the tofu on the baking tray and sprinkle with 1 tablespoon of the soy sauce and the chile oil. Cook in a preheated oven at 400°F for 20 minutes. Heat the safflower and sesame oils in a wok or skillet. Add the carrots and mushrooms and cook for a few minutes until tender, but still with some bite to them. Add the hoisin, the remaining 1 tablespoon soy sauce, the rice vinegar, and about ¾ cup water. Continue cooking for 2 minutes. Stir in the scallions, roasted tofu, and salt and pepper to taste.

Using a separate wok or a large skillet, stir-fry the bok choy for 2–3 minutes, until cooked but still a little crunchy.

Put 3 patties on each plate, with a mound of bok choy and the tofu and mushrooms spooned alongside. Sprinkle chopped cilantro over the top and serve.

COOK'S TIP

I like to use deep-fried rather than plain tofu because the texture, flavor, and appearance is enhanced by the frying process. Tofu is available from natural food stores already fried, or it is easy to fry your own. Heat the oil and put the cubes of firm tofu in the oil until they swell up. Alternatively, the tofu could be first marinated, then deep-fried to get the maximum flavor possible.

mango and lime tart brûlée

1 cup sugar

4 eggs

1 cup heavy cream

¾ cup mango pulp, canned or fresh and puréed (about 1 large ripe mango)

freshly squeezed juice of 2 limes and 1 teaspoon freshly grated zest of unwaxed lime

2 tablespoons brown sugar, for sprinkling

whipped cream or crème fraîche, to serve

SWEET SHORTCRUST PASTRY DOUGH

1 lb. all-purpose flour (sifted if you have time)

a pinch of salt

4 oz. cold butter, cut into cubes

3 tablespoons sugar

a tart pan with removable bottom, 12-inches diameter

parchment paper and baking beans, small weights, or rice

SERVES 6–8

I'm not really a great dessert eater, but I love this one because I'm a huge fan of mango. This is an impressive-looking tart that can be rustled up effortlessly. In fact, you can make it the day before and do the "brûlée" topping just before serving.

To make the dough, put the flour and salt into a bowl, then put the butter cubes in the middle. Using your fingertips, rub the butter lightly into the flour until the dough looks like bread crumbs. Stir in the sugar and enough cold water for form a soft but not sticky dough. Cover with plastic wrap and chill for 30 minutes.

Roll out the dough to fit the pan, drape it over a rolling pin, then drape the pin over the tart pan. Press the dough into the corners, then roll the pin over the top to trim off the excess. Prick a few holes in the base, then line with parchment paper and fill with baking beans or small weights to prevent the dough from rising. Bake in a preheated oven at 350°F for 10 minutes (this is called blind baking). Gently remove the baking beans and parchment, then return to the oven to cook for a further 10 minutes or until lightly golden. Remove from the oven and let cool.

Put the sugar, eggs, and cream in a bowl and beat with electric beaters. Stir in the mango, lime juice, and zest. Pour into the pie crust and bake for 30 minutes or until the tart is just starting to set. Remove from the oven and let cool.

Sprinkle brown sugar over the top and either put the tart under a preheated broiler or use a cook's blowtorch to melt the sugar until it is molten and bubbling.

Serve with whipped cream or crème fraîche.

COOK'S TIP

The quality of the dough will depend on keeping the ingredients cold—the butter, water, and ideally, hands! There is no shame in using good-quality store-bought dough if you can find it where you live. Fresh ready-made dough is preferable to the frozen sort.

OUTDOOR GRILLS

portobello mushrooms
with lemon and olive oil

4 large portobello
mushrooms, about 8 oz.

MARINADE

2 tablespoons olive oil

1 tablespoon soy sauce

grated zest and juice
of 1 unwaxed lemon

2 garlic cloves, crushed

4 sprigs of rosemary

freshly ground
black pepper

TO SERVE

crusty bread

horseradish sauce

SERVES 4

The earthy, almost meaty flavor of portobello mushrooms needs very little to improve it. Simple cooking and a complement of good-quality ingredients will reveal their absolute best.

To make the marinade, put the olive oil, soy sauce, lemon zest and juice, garlic, rosemary, and pepper in a bowl, mix well, then pour over the mushrooms so that they are well covered. Set aside to infuse for 30 minutes.

Put the mushrooms on the preheated grill or stove-top grill pan and cook for 5 minutes on each side or until softened.

Serve the mushrooms on top of crusty bread with a smear of horseradish, then pour any remaining marinade juices over the top.

eggplant and smoked cheese rolls

2 eggplant, cut lengthwise into about 5 slices each

1 teaspoon chile oil

½ cup olive oil

1 tablespoon cumin seeds, lightly toasted in a dry skillet and ground

2 garlic cloves, crushed

1 red chile, seeded and finely chopped

a large handful of mint leaves, finely chopped

8 oz. firm smoked cheese, sliced

sea salt and freshly ground black pepper

TO SERVE

a large handful of cilantro, coarsely chopped

freshly squeezed juice of ½ lemon

MAKES 10 ROLLS

I have a deep love affair with eggplant and have to resist the temptation to put them in everything—but it isn't easy! Truly at home in both Middle Eastern and Mediterranean cuisines, they are compatible with endless spices, herbs, and a multitude of other ingredients. In this dish, they soak up the fragrance of spices and are paired with smoked cheese, enhancing the already smoky grilled flavor.

Arrange the eggplant slices on a large tray. Mix the chile and olive oils, cumin, garlic, chile, mint, salt, and pepper in a measuring cup, then pour over the eggplant. Turn each slice over so that both sides are well coated. Cover with plastic wrap and set aside for a few hours or overnight to soak up all the flavors.

Put the eggplant on a preheated grill or smoking-hot stove-top grill pan. Cook for about 4 minutes, then turn and cook the other side until tender and browned.

Remove from the heat, put some of the cheese at one end of an eggplant slice and roll up firmly (do this while the eggplant is still hot so the cheese melts). Repeat with the other slices. Sprinkle with the cilantro and lemon juice, then serve.

asparagus and lemon
with smoked garlic mayonnaise

I look forward to the arrival of asparagus each year because it means that summer is just around the corner. The beauty of this vegetable is that it needs very little to go with it—just something for dunking! I believe that to roast or grill asparagus is to enjoy it at its best. If using a charcoal grill, start cooking when the coals turn white, since this is when they are at their hottest. If using a stove-top grill pan, start cooking when the pan is smoking hot to maximize the asparagus flavor.

16 asparagus spears

2–3 tablespoons olive oil

sea salt and freshly ground black pepper

freshly squeezed juice of 1/2 lemon, to serve

SMOKED GARLIC MAYONNAISE

3–4 smoked garlic cloves, crushed

1/4 cup mayonnaise

SERVES 4

Heat the grill or stove-top grill pan until very hot.

Put the asparagus in a bowl, add the olive oil, and toss to coat. Set on the hot grill or pan and cook for about 10 minutes, turning frequently, or until starting to become golden brown. Remove to a plate and sprinkle with salt and pepper. Squeeze the lemon juice over the top before serving.

Stir the smoked garlic into the mayonnaise and serve as the perfect accompaniment to the hot lemony fingers of asparagus.

COOK'S TIP

To prepare asparagus, just snap off and discard the woody ends (they snap naturally in the right place).

2 red Cubanelle peppers, halved lengthwise and seeded, or bell peppers

4 slices of ciabatta bread, thickly cut diagonally

1 garlic clove

2–3 tablespoons olive oil

sea salt

torn basil leaves, to serve

SERVES 5

Put the peppers on a preheated grill or stove-top grill pan, then cook until the skins have blackened. Remove the skins.

Remove the peppers, then toast the bread on both sides, taking care that it does not burn. Rub each side with the garlic clove.

Put the bread on a plate and sprinkle generously with olive oil and sea salt. Top with the pepper and basil and serve.

COOK'S TIP

Cubanelle peppers (see page 91) are the shape of a huge chile, but rather than being hot, they are incredibly sweet. Roasting bell peppers, or any vegetable for that matter, intensifies the natural sweetness—using Cubanelles means that you are at an advantage before you even start. They are available in red, yellow, and orange and look supremely pretty served together. If you can't find them, use regular bell peppers.

grilled bread with cubanelle peppers

This is a sophisticated open sandwich, with the sweetness of the roasted Cubanelle peppers complementing the garlicky bread. As a variation, bruschetta is always good: grill the bread, rub with a raw garlic clove, sprinkle with olive oil, then squeeze half a tomato over the bread, discarding the skin. Top with slices of avocado for something a little more substantial.

8 oz. firm tofu

2 tablespoons hoisin sauce

3 tablespoons soy sauce

1 red serrano chile, finely chopped

1 inch fresh ginger, peeled and grated

1 teaspoon toasted sesame oil

1 tablespoon rice vinegar

a handful of cilantro, coarsely chopped, to serve

SERVES 4

tofu in a hot, sweet, spicy infusion

Tofu receives some bad press and even I agree that it can be exceedingly dull and tasteless when served *au naturel*. However, it does act as a sponge for marinades. The flavors percolate all the way through, giving the tofu a fantastic extra lease of life and great versatility. For vegetarians, it is a good source of protein and, for meat-eaters, a welcome fat-free alternative.

Cut through the cake of tofu horizontally to make 2 thin slices. Cut each slice into 4 pieces.

Put the hoisin, soy sauce, chile, ginger, sesame oil, and rice vinegar in a bowl and mix well. Pour onto a large plate, then put the tofu on top. Spoon some of the mixture over the top so that the tofu is completely covered. Leave for as long as possible to soak up the flavors, at least 2 hours or overnight.

When ready to cook, put the tofu on a preheated grill or smoking-hot stove-top grill pan, reserving some of the marinade. Cook each side for 4–5 minutes until lightly browned. Serve immediately with the reserved marinade, topped with cilantro.

zucchini and patty pans

infused with mint and balsamic vinegar

If you think that grilled food is predictable, this dish will change your opinion and prove to be a refreshing change. It looks and tastes sunny and fresh—you can prepare it before the guests arrive, then leave it to soak up the oil, mint, and balsamic vinegar. Delicious.

Put the patty pans on a preheated grill or stove-top grill pan. Cook on each side for about 5 minutes or until tender, turning over when starting to brown.

When cooked, transfer to a long serving dish. Pour over the oil and vinegar and sprinkle with pine nuts, mint, salt, and pepper.

Cook the sliced zucchini on the grill or in the pan for just 1–2 minutes each side. Add to the patty pan mixture and turn to coat. Cover and marinate for about 2 hours in the refrigerator, then serve.

COOK'S TIP

Patty pans are members of the squash family and are either yellow or green. They look a little alien, rather like mini flying saucers, but taste wonderful. They are available from large supermarkets all summer.

1 lb. yellow and green baby patty pan squashes, cut in half (or extra zucchini)

1/3 cup olive oil

2 tablespoons balsamic vinegar

3/4 cup pine nuts, about 2 oz., lightly toasted in a dry skillet

a handful of fresh mint leaves, coarsely chopped

3 zucchini (about 1 lb.), cut lengthwise into 1/8-inch slices

sea salt and freshly ground black pepper

SERVES 4

tuscan bread salad

The success of this simple and authentic Italian recipe depends on the finest quality olive oil. It will largely dictate the aroma and flavor of the salad. Use it generously, and don't worry about the calories—olive oil is a completely natural food, rich in the antioxidants and vitamins that help prevent body cells aging. How many other foods can boast that!

Put the bread in a large bowl and mix in the oil, vinegar, lemon juice, garlic, and 2 tablespoons water, mashing the bread a little with a fork as you go. Stir in the tomatoes, cucumber, onion, capers, and basil. Season with salt and pepper and serve.

COOK'S TIP

The salad can be made in advance but must be eaten on the same day. Add the basil just before serving to keep its vibrant color.

8 oz. ciabatta bread, cut into very small cubes

½ cup extra virgin olive oil

2 tablespoons sherry vinegar (or use balsamic or red wine vinegar)

1 tablespoon lemon juice

1 garlic clove, crushed

2 beefsteak tomatoes (about 10 oz.), cut into tiny cubes

½ cucumber, halved, seeded, and cut into small squares

1 red onion, finely chopped

¼ cup capers, rinsed and drained, or caperberries

a large bunch of fresh basil leaves, torn

sea salt and freshly ground black pepper

SERVES 4

plantain with lime and chile

Plantain lends itself very well to grills and grill pans. The cooking process brings out its sweetness, so it's good to offset that with a bit of citrus and chile. It always amazes me that some people are unfamiliar with this gorgeous vegetable, which is readily available from some supermarkets or specialty Caribbean shops. It is also great shallow-fried with sweet chile sauce served on the side.

2 plantains (*plátanos maduros*), thinly sliced diagonally

freshly squeezed juice of 1 lime

1 tablespoon chile oil

sea salt

coarsely chopped cilantro, to serve

SERVES 4

Put the slices of plantain in a large bowl with the lime juice and chile oil. Carefully turn them over to cover evenly (this will stop them discoloring).

Arrange the slices on a preheated grill or stove-top grill pan and cook for 2–3 minutes or until slightly browned. Gently turn them over, using a spatula, then cook the other side for 2 minutes. (The plantain changes from a fleshy color to a beautiful bright yellow blackened with the stripes of the pan or grill.)

When cooked, lift onto a plate, sprinkle with salt and cilantro and serve.

COOK'S TIP

When plantains are ripe and at their best for cooking, they have blackened skins and look like ordinary bananas that have gone past their best.

DILL POLENTA

3 tablespoons unsalted butter

1 tablespoon olive oil

1½ cups polenta or yellow cornmeal, about 8 oz.

1½ oz. fresh Parmesan cheese, grated

a handful of fresh dill, coarsely chopped

sea salt and freshly ground black pepper

MARINATED FENNEL

2 tablespoons sherry or red wine vinegar

3 tablespoons olive oil

2 garlic cloves, crushed

2 bulbs of fennel, tough outer leaves removed, remainder sliced

sea salt and freshly ground black pepper

MARINATED SCALLIONS

8 scallions

1 tablespoon sherry or red wine vinegar

1 tablespoon olive oil

sea salt and freshly ground black pepper

TO SERVE

1½ oz. fresh Parmesan cheese, grated

grated zest of ½ unwaxed lemon

sea salt

a jelly roll pan, 12 x 10 inches, lightly greased

a cookie cutter, 3½-inches diameter

SERVES 4

lemon, fennel, and scallions
on grilled dill polenta

There are three ingredients I think fennel should never be without—lemon, olive oil, and dill. If you don't have any fresh dill, chop up the feathery fronds from the top of the fennel and use as a replacement. The polenta is used instead of bread and provides a good base for the flavors of the dish.

To make the polenta, melt the butter and oil in a medium saucepan. Add 5 cups water and bring to a boil. Pour in the polenta in a steady stream, beating all the time. Continue to cook according to the instructions on the package, until the grainy texture has disappeared. Stir in the Parmesan, dill, salt, and pepper. Spoon into the prepared jelly roll pan, then let cool until firm.

To marinate the fennel, put the vinegar, oil, garlic, salt, and pepper in a bowl and mix well. Add the fennel and set aside to develop the flavors.

Put the scallions, vinegar, oil, salt, and pepper in a separate bowl and set aside to marinate.

Cut out rounds of polenta with the cookie cutter. Cook on a preheated grill or stove-top grill pan for 5 minutes on each side, until browned.

Add the fennel to the grill or pan. Cook for 5–10 minutes until browned on both sides and tender. While the fennel is cooking, add the scallions and cook for 2–3 minutes until lightly blackened.

Serve the polenta piled high with fennel and scallions and sprinkle with Parmesan, lemon zest, and sea salt. Pour any remaining marinade juices over the top.

grilled pineapple
with coconut, chile, and lime ice cream

Pineapple, coconut, and lime juice—are these not the flavors of a tropical heatwave? OK, so the chile may seem a little avant-garde, but it works! The cream and coconut diffuse the heat of the chile so that all that remains is its taste, texture, and color—providing a flash of red on white, and making a thoroughly intriguing combination.

1 pineapple, peeled, cored, and cut into 1-inch slices

1 tablespoon unsalted butter (if using a grill pan)

confectioners' sugar, to dust

COCONUT, CHILE, AND LIME ICE CREAM

1 cup canned coconut milk

1 cup heavy cream

⅓ cup sugar

grated zest of 2 unwaxed limes and freshly squeezed juice of 1 lime

½ large red chile, seeded and finely chopped

SERVES 4

To make the ice cream, put the coconut milk, cream, and sugar in a saucepan. Heat gently until the sugar has dissolved. Let cool, then add the lime zest, lime juice, and chile. Transfer to an ice cream maker and churn according to the manufacturer's instructions, or pour into a rigid covered container and freeze for 1½–2 hours until the ice cream has set about 1 inch from the edge. Beat to break down the larger crystals, then return to the freezer for a further 4 hours or overnight.

Preheat the grill or stove-top grill pan. If using the grill pan, add the butter and melt, to prevent the pineapple from sticking. Add the pineapple and cook for 5 minutes on each side, until slightly charred.

Dust the pineapple with confectioners' sugar and serve with scoops of the ice cream.

banana packages with chocolate and rum

Ever so slightly decadent, this is a dish to help you recreate the taste of the Caribbean in minutes. Equally good cooked outside on a grill in the heat of summer or made on a stove-top grill pan in the depths of winter.

4 banana leaves or aluminum foil, cut to 10 inches square

4 bananas, halved crosswise

4 oz. dark chocolate, broken into small pieces

¼ cup dark rum

1 tablespoon safflower oil (if using a grill pan)

whipped cream, to serve

twine or raffia, soaked in water for 15 minutes

SERVES 4

Put the banana leaves on a work surface. On the first leaf, put 2 banana halves side by side. Sprinkle with one-quarter of the chocolate and 1 tablespoon rum. Fold up the sides and edges to form a square package. Tie with the wet twine or raffia (soaking will prevent the twine from burning). Repeat to make 4 packages.

Put the packages on a preheated grill or oiled, smoking-hot stove-top grill pan and cook for about 10 minutes on each side.

Snip the twine and serve with whipped cream.

COOK'S TIP

Banana leaves are available from Latin-American markets and Asian stores. To make them more malleable, put on the grill or grill pan for 1 minute before using. Aluminum foil makes a worthy substitute.

So, it's a family meal for eight with one vegetarian. The aim is to produce delicious food but to simplify time spent in the kitchen. However, you don't want the token vegetarian to stand out as a "special needs" guest with an isolated menu. What would be perfect is a dish which would also serve as a complement to the meat. Here are four vegetarian dishes that work very well with meat options.

SUNDAY LUNCHES and FAMILY DINNERS

roasted vegetable dauphinois

This rich, creamy, garlicky sauce is offset by the earthy flavors of root vegetables, plus the slightly tart and highly aromatic sage. It is incredibly straightforward to prepare, and non-vegetarians will love it just as much—it's delicious with lamb. Serve with lemon-roasted potatoes and a herby leaf salad with mustard dressing.

1 garlic clove

butter, softened,
for brushing

1 lb. parsnips, cut into
$\frac{1}{2}$-inch diagonal slices

a handful of fresh
sage leaves

12 oz. carrots, cut into
$\frac{1}{2}$-inch diagonal slices

12 oz. uncooked
unpeeled beets,
scrubbed well and cut
into $\frac{1}{2}$-inch diagonal
slices

1$\frac{1}{4}$ cups heavy cream

1 tablespoon olive oil

sea salt and freshly
ground black pepper

*a baking dish, about
12 inches square*

SERVES 4

Rub the garlic around the base and sides of the baking dish, then brush with butter. Pack overlapping slices of parsnips into the dish. Season well with salt and pepper, then add one-third of the sage leaves.

Repeat the process, first with the carrots, then the beets, seasoning each layer with salt and pepper and dotting with the remaining sage. Pour in the cream.

Cover the dish with foil and bake in a preheated oven at 400°F for 1 hour 40 minutes. Remove the foil and lightly sprinkle the top with the olive oil. Return to the oven and continue cooking for a further 20 minutes or until the vegetables are very tender.

red onion and taleggio tart

If you want to create a self-contained package of food that can be slotted in as a replacement to meat, this tart is perfect. It can be prepared at the last minute, so it makes a good emergency standby. You can substitute rosemary and Camembert for the richer Italian Taleggio if preferred. Serve as a vegetable accompaniment for meat-eaters in the family, and as an entrée for vegetarians. Ratatouille and green beans tossed in garlic and olive oil for everyone.

12 oz. puff pastry dough

all-purpose flour, for dusting

$1/2$ tablespoon olive oil

3 tablespoons unsalted butter

3 red onions, halved lengthwise, then sliced lengthwise into crescents

$1/2$ cup red wine

1 tablespoon sherry vinegar

1 tablespoon brown sugar

$1^1/2$ oz. Taleggio cheese, sliced

$1/4$ cup fresh thyme leaves

sea salt and freshly ground black pepper

a cookie cutter, 5 inches diameter

a baking tray, lightly greased

SERVES 4

Roll out the dough on a floured work surface and cut out 4 rounds using the cookie cutter. Set them on the prepared baking tray.

Put the olive oil and 2 tablespoons of the butter in a medium saucepan and melt over low heat. Add the onions and cook slowly for 10 minutes until very soft. Stir in the red wine, sherry vinegar, and brown sugar. Continue cooking for 10 minutes, then add salt and pepper to taste.

Spoon the mixture onto the dough rounds, leaving a 1-inch border around the edges. Melt the remaining butter and use to brush the edges. Put the Taleggio on top of the onion and sprinkle with the thyme. Bake in a preheated oven at 350°F for 15–20 minutes until the crust is golden and well risen. Eat hot or cold.

butternut squash and goat cheese layers

These layers of sweet orange squash and molten cheese provide a truly stunning focal point to any meal. Try them with slow-cooked red cabbage, juniper, and chile, plus potato mashed with scallions on the side. A mixed green salad could be substituted for the mashed potatoes, since the butternut squash and goat cheese is deceptively filling. For meat-eaters in the family, this dish goes well with roast pork.

2 butternut squash

4 oz. fresh goat cheese, crumbled

1 cup fresh bread crumbs

$\frac{1}{4}$ cup thick Greek-style yogurt

1 tablespoon fresh marjoram leaves

1 tablespoon fresh thyme leaves

olive oil, for sprinkling

sea salt and freshly ground black pepper

paprika, to serve

a baking tray, lightly greased

SERVES 4: MAKES
ABOUT 8 STACKS

Cut the long, seedless section of squash into 1-inch rings. Reserve the bulbous part for another use. Peel the rings, then cook them in boiling salted water for 10 minutes, or until tender. Drain.

Put the goat cheese, bread crumbs, yogurt, herbs, salt, and pepper in a bowl and mix.

Put 4 rounds of squash on the baking tray, top with some of the cheese mixture, then with another round of squash, finishing with some more cheese. Repeat until you have used up all the squash and cheese.

Sprinkle the top of each stack with olive oil and bake in a preheated oven at 400°F for 30 minutes. Serve 2 stacks each, sprinkled with a little paprika.

toad in the hole
with red onion gravy

A true English classic—sausages baked in a light, fluffy batter—is given an extra twist with red bell pepper and thyme. The dish is perfect for vegetarian friends and is wonderful served with roast beef as an alternative to Yorkshire puddings. Add roast potatoes, sweet roasted parsnips, and buttery stir-fried cabbage, with the red onion gravy as the final touch. What could be better?

Cook the sausages according to the instructions on the package. When cooked, cut them in half crosswise.

To make the batter, put the flour and salt in a bowl. Make a well in the center and add the beaten eggs. Beat vigorously, adding the milk as you go, until the mixture is smooth. Put in the refrigerator to rest for 30 minutes.

Meanwhile, to make the gravy, put the onions in a saucepan and add the butter, oil, and rosemary. Cook over low heat for 10–15 minutes, until they start to caramelize, but not brown. Stir in the flour and continue cooking over low heat for a further 2–3 minutes. Add the sugar and wine and cook for 5 minutes. Slowly stir in the stock, bring to a boil, and add salt and pepper to taste. Keep the gravy over low heat until ready to serve.

Pour about ⅛-inch of oil into 8 of the cups in the muffin tray. Heat in a preheated oven at 475°F for about 10 minutes, or until the pan and oil are very hot. Spoon the batter into the cups, then put 2 sausage halves and some red pepper in each cup. Sprinkle the thyme on top.

Put the muffin trays on a baking tray and bake for 25 minutes until golden and well risen. Serve with a sprinkle of salt and a spoonful of red onion gravy.

8 vegetarian sausages

¾ cup all-purpose flour

a pinch of sea salt

3 eggs, lightly beaten

1 cup plus 1 tablespoon milk

½ red bell pepper, halved, seeded, and thinly sliced

a few fresh thyme leaves

sea salt, to serve

safflower oil, for cooking

RED ONION GRAVY

2 red onions, halved and thinly sliced

2 tablespoons unsalted butter

1 teaspoon olive oil

leaves from a sprig of rosemary

1 tablespoon all-purpose flour

1 tablespoon brown sugar

1 cup red wine

2 cups vegetable stock

sea salt and freshly ground black pepper

2 muffin trays, 6 cups each, 3-inches diameter

a baking tray

SERVES 4

SUMMER ENTERTAINING

2 eggplant, cut lengthwise into about 6 slices

olive oil, for brushing

RED BELL PEPPER SAUCE

2 red bell peppers, halved and seeded

1 tablespoon olive oil, plus extra for sprinkling

1 teaspoon balsamic vinegar

sea salt and freshly ground black pepper

PESTO RISOTTO

4 tablespoons unsalted butter

1 tablespoon olive oil

1 onion, finely chopped

1 cup risotto rice, such as arborio

1 quart hot vegetable stock

2 tablespoons pesto

4 oz. freshly grated Parmesan cheese

sea salt and freshly ground black pepper

TO SERVE

whole basil leaves

Parmesan cheese, shaved with a vegetable peeler

2–3 baking trays

SERVES 4

eggplant rolls with pesto risotto

Sculptural, robust, and unfussy, this dish radiates the freshness and brightness of good food. The three colors of deep purple, green, and red offer a delicious combination to enjoy. Excellent served with a simple green salad.

Arrange the slices of eggplant on a baking tray and lightly brush with olive oil (they can also be broiled or cooked in a stove-top grill pan, if you prefer). Bake in a preheated oven at 400°F for 10–15 minutes until tender but not so soft that they fall apart. Remove from the oven, sprinkle with the balsamic vinegar, and transfer to a plate.

Put the bell peppers on the baking tray, sprinkle with olive oil, and roast for 20–30 minutes until the skins have lightly blackened and the flesh is soft. Carefully remove the skins.

Meanwhile, to make the risotto, put the butter and oil in a wide saucepan and melt over medium heat. Add the onion and sauté for 10 minutes until soft. Stir in the rice, letting it soak up all the buttery juices. Add the hot stock, a ladle at a time, stirring constantly and letting the rice absorb the liquid between additions. This will take 15–20 minutes, and the rice should be cooked but still retain a little bite. Stir in the pesto and Parmesan and add salt and pepper to taste. The rice can be cooled, or used hot.

To assemble the rolls, put a spoonful of risotto at the narrow end of each slice of eggplant. Roll up firmly and put seam side down on the baking tray. Repeat until all the ingredients have been used. Cover the tray with foil and bake for 15 minutes until the eggplant and rice are heated through.

To complete the pepper sauce, put the roasted bell peppers and the tablespoon of olive oil in a food processor and blend until smooth. Stir in the balsamic vinegar and add salt and pepper to taste.

To serve, put spoonfuls of the sauce on plates, add the rolls, and top with whole basil leaves and shavings of Parmesan.

1 tablespoon olive oil

½ onion, finely chopped

1 green bell pepper, seeded and finely chopped

½ green serrano chile, seeded and finely chopped

6 cups vegetable stock

freshly squeezed juice of 1 lime

1 avocado, halved and pitted

a handful of fresh mint leaves

sea salt and freshly ground black pepper

TO SERVE

plain yogurt

crushed ice

SERVES 4

Put the oil, onion, bell pepper, and chile in a saucepan and cook over gentle heat for about 20 minutes until completely soft. Let cool.

Transfer to a blender, add the vegetable stock, lime juice, avocado, and mint leaves, and purée until smooth. Add salt and pepper to taste, then serve in bowls or glasses, topped with a spoonful of yogurt and some crushed ice.

I think there's nothing better than a cold soup on a hot summer's day! The secret is to make it look gorgeous while keeping the portions small. Glasses are a great idea for serving, showing off the vibrant green color—utterly seductive.

chilled avocado and pepper soup

feta salad with sugar snaps

and minty yogurt dressing

6 oz. sugar snap peas

8 oz. green beans, stems removed

8 oz. feta cheese, cut into small squares

½ cucumber, halved lengthwise, seeded, and sliced diagonally

a handful of fresh mint leaves, finely chopped

1 red chile, seeded and finely chopped

sea salt

YOGURT DRESSING

3 tablespoons Greek-style yogurt

1 tablespoon olive oil

1 tablespoon lemon juice

SERVES 4

I really enjoy the balance of flavors and sensations in this salad. The heat of the chile, the cool of the yogurt and cucumber, together with the saltiness of the feta make it just perfect for summer dining.

Bring a large saucepan of salted water to a boil, plunge in the sugar snaps, and cook briefly until they turn bright green, about 30 seconds. Remove with a slotted spoon and transfer to a bowl of cold water.

Return to a boil, then add the beans and cook for 4 minutes until tender. Drain in a colander and refresh under cold running water.

To make the dressing, put the yogurt, olive oil, and lemon juice in a small bowl and beat well.

Put the feta in a large bowl, add the sugar snaps, beans, cucumber, and mint. Pour the dressing over the salad, toss well, then serve topped with the chile.

I like nothing better than eating good bread with a dip and my favorite vegetable—eggplant. Give yourself plenty of time to make the bread. And try to time the last batch of baking so that the aromas leave your guests in no doubt that the bread is homemade. Serve with a salad of tomatoes, red onions, and herbs.

cilantro flatbreads
with spiced eggplant and split pea dip

CILANTRO FLATBREADS

5 cups white bread flour, plus extra for dusting

¼ oz. package active dry yeast

2 teaspoons sea salt

1 tablespoon cumin seeds, lightly toasted in a dry skillet

a large handful of cilantro, chopped

1 red serrano chile, seeded and finely chopped

about 4 cups warm water

olive oil, for brushing

SPICED EGGPLANT

freshly squeezed juice of 1 lemon

1 red serrano chile, seeded and chopped

a large handful of fresh mint leaves, finely chopped

½ cup olive oil

3 eggplant, cut into chunks

1 red onion, cut into wedges

flat-leaf parsley

sea salt and freshly ground black pepper

SPLIT PEA DIP

2 cups yellow split peas, about 10 oz.

1 teaspoon cumin seeds, lightly toasted in a dry skillet, then ground in a coffee grinder

freshly squeezed juice of 1 lemon

2 garlic cloves, crushed

¼ cup olive oil, plus extra to serve

a handful of fresh dill, coarsely chopped

sea salt and freshly ground black pepper

1–2 large baking trays, lightly greased

SERVES 4

To make the flatbreads, put the flour in a large bowl, then stir in the yeast, salt, cumin seeds, cilantro, and chile. Make a well in the center and add the water. Mix with your hands to form a dough. Either transfer to an electric mixer fitted with a dough hook or continue kneading by hand on a lightly floured surface for about 10 minutes or until the dough is smooth and springy to the touch. Return to the bowl, lightly brush the top with oil, then cover with plastic wrap. Let rise in a warm place for 30–40 minutes.

To make the spiced eggplant, put the lemon juice, chile, mint, olive oil, 1 teaspoon salt, and pepper in a blender and process until smooth. Put the eggplant and red onions on the baking tray. Pour the olive oil mixture over the vegetables and massage in well with your hands. Bake in a preheated oven at 400°F for 30 minutes, then transfer to a serving bowl and top with the parsley.

To make the dip, put the yellow split peas in a medium saucepan, then cover with cold water and add 1 teaspoon salt. Bring to a boil and cook for 30–40 minutes until soft. Drain, then transfer to a food processor. Add the cumin, lemon juice, garlic, and olive oil and blend to a smooth purée. Add salt and pepper to taste, then transfer to a bowl and sprinkle with extra olive oil and some dill.

Meanwhile, to cook the flatbreads, transfer the dough to a lightly floured work surface and knead for a few minutes. Divide into 20–25 balls. Using a rolling pin, roll the dough balls into thin, flat ovals. Put on a lightly greased baking tray and cook in batches in a preheated oven at 450°F for 15–20 minutes until golden and puffy.

Serve the flatbreads with the spiced eggplant and dip.

summer brioche dessert

4 small individual brioches

1 lb. fresh or frozen and thawed summer berries

¼ cup sugar

thick whipped cream or crème fraîche, to serve

SERVES 4

This superb dessert doesn't really have to be eaten solely in summer. I have used a bag of frozen berries which works just as well as the fresh fruit, so this delicious recipe can be enjoyed all year round.

Carefully trim the tops off the brioches and reserve as the lids. Using a small, sharp knife, cut out a large cavity in the middle of each brioche.

Put the fruit and sugar in a saucepan and heat gently until the sugar has dissolved. Dip the brioche lids into the liquid, then start spooning the fruit into the cavity. (It looks like a lot but the brioche will soak up all the fruit and juices.) Put the lids on top at a jaunty angle and chill in the refrigerator for at least 3 hours.

Serve with cream.

pan-grilled strawberries

with black pepper ice cream

Strawberries and black pepper make an unusual but famous food combination that really works. Strawberries with ice cream are also a match made in heaven, so why not combine the two ideas? I think it's fabulous and certainly proves to be a great topic of discussion among guests. The slight heat from the pepper hits the tastebuds last and marries beautifully with the sweet fruit.

1 tablespoon unsalted butter

8 oz. strawberries, left whole with green stems

confectioners' sugar, for sprinkling

PEPPER ICE CREAM

½ cup sugar

4 oz. mascarpone cheese

½ cup Greek-style yogurt

2 teaspoons freshly ground black pepper

an ice cream maker or freezer-proof container

SERVES 4

To make the ice cream, put the sugar and 1 cup water in a small saucepan and heat gently until the sugar has dissolved. Let cool. Put the mascarpone, yogurt, and black pepper in a bowl and beat well. Using a balloon whisk, beat the creamy mixture into the cooled sweet liquid.

Transfer to an ice cream maker and continue according to the manufacturer's instructions. Alternatively, transfer into a rigid container and freeze for 1½–2 hours, or until the mixture has set about 1 inch from the edge. Beat to break down the larger crystals, then return to the freezer for 4 hours or overnight. Remove from the freezer 15 minutes before serving to soften.

To cook the strawberries, preheat a stove-top grill pan. Add the butter and, when melted, add the strawberries. Press lightly onto the pan so they are branded with dark lines. Turn them over and do the same on the other side. Serve immediately, with a dusting of confectioners' sugar and a scoop of black pepper ice cream.

COOK'S TIP

Do not overcook the strawberries—the idea is that they remain firm with only the outsides slightly softened by the heat.

WINTER ENTERTAINING

italian borlotti beans and farro

Borlotti beans are one of Italy's most popular beans, plump and speckled with magenta and gray. When cooked, they become creamy and slightly nutty in flavor, and serve as the perfect partner to the chewy textured spelt, which is often referred to simply as *farro*. If you can't find borlotti, use pinto beans or pink beans. This dish, inspired by Gabi Matzeu, is a substantial meal—a comforting winter recipe and highly nutritious. All it needs as a partner is a leafy salad or lightly steamed greens.

3 tablespoons olive oil

3 carrots, cut into small cubes

3 celery stalks, very finely chopped

1 large onion, finely chopped

2 garlic cloves, crushed

1¾ cups borlotti beans, about 10 oz., soaked overnight, drained, then cooked for 1–1½ hours until tender (reserving 1¾ cups of the cooking liquid)

1¼ cups organic farro

1 quart vegetable stock

sea salt and freshly ground black pepper

shavings of fresh Parmesan cheese, to serve

SERVES 4

Put the olive oil, carrots, celery, onion, and garlic in a saucepan and cook gently until soft. Press the beans and reserved bean liquor through a food mill or strainer into the vegetable mixture. This removes the bean skins, giving a smoother consistency and making the beans more digestible. Alternatively, transfer to a food processor and blend to a coarse purée.

Stir in the spelt and stock, cover with a lid, and cook gently for about 1 hour, stirring frequently, until thickened (the longer the cooking time the thicker the consistency). Add salt and pepper to taste and serve topped with shaved Parmesan.

thyme and red onion soup

with goat cheese crouton

There is something about the sweetness of red onions contrasting with the slight tartness of goat cheese that proves irresistible every time. The soup can be served as a meal in itself for lunch or as a substantial entrée for dinner.

Put the olive oil, onions, and thyme in a large saucepan. Cook over gentle heat for about 15 minutes until the onion is very soft. Stir in the stock, red wine, sugar, and vinegar. Bring just to the boiling point—but do not let it boil.

Meanwhile, put the bread under the broiler. Toast 1 side, then put the cheese on the untoasted side and broil until melting.

Mix the cornstarch with 1 tablespoon water to form a paste. Slowly add to the soup, stirring all the time, until glossy and thickened. Season with salt and pepper.

Serve the soup hot with a cheese crouton floating in each bowl.

VARIATION

Serve crusty bread on the side and crumble the goat cheese over the soup.

2 tablespoons olive oil

3 red onions, quartered then very finely sliced

1 tablespoon fresh thyme leaves

1½ quarts vegetable stock

¾ cup red wine

2 tablespoons brown sugar

2 tablespoons balsamic vinegar

1 tablespoon cornstarch

sea salt and freshly ground black pepper

CHEESE CROUTONS

4 slices French bread

4 oz. goat cheese, cut into 4 pieces

SERVES 4

5 shallots, chopped

3 stalks of lemongrass, outer leaves removed, white bulb very thinly sliced

3 lime leaves, or 1 teaspoon grated lime zest

1 inch fresh galangal or ginger, coarsely chopped

1 inch fresh ginger, peeled and grated

freshly squeezed juice of 1 lime

1¾ cups canned coconut milk

1 tablespoon soy sauce

4 teaspoons tom yam paste (see Cook's Tip)

8 oz. canned bamboo shoots, drained

8 oz. canned water chestnuts, drained

1 tablespoon safflower oil

1 large bok choy, thickly sliced

½ white cabbage (about 12 oz.), cored and thinly sliced

4 oz. spinach, thinly sliced

2½ cups bean sprouts, about 10 oz., rinsed and drained

a large handful of cilantro, coarsely chopped

sea salt and freshly ground black pepper

SCENTED RICE

1 cup fragrant Thai rice, such as jasmine

½ teaspoon ground turmeric

1 stalk of lemongrass, cut into 3 pieces

½ teaspoon sea salt

PAPAYA SALAD

⅔ cup raw, unsalted peanuts

1 tablespoon soy sauce

3 green, unripe papaya, peeled, halved, and seeded

freshly squeezed juice of 3 limes

1 red serrano chile, seeded and finely chopped

a large handful of cilantro, coarsely chopped

SERVES 4

thai curry with scented rice

and spicy papaya salad

This dish has beautiful and lively flavors that dance on the palate. Visually the colors are warm and tropical, so it is especially good in the depths of winter when your guests are wistfully thinking of warmer climates.

Put the shallots, lemongrass, lime leaves, galangal, ginger, lime juice, and half the coconut milk in a blender. Process to a smooth paste. Transfer to a medium saucepan and add the soy sauce, tom yam paste, bamboo shoots, water chestnuts, and the remaining coconut milk. Cook over gentle heat for about 20 minutes to develop the flavors.

Cook the rice with the turmeric, lemongrass, and salt, according to the instructions on the package. Discard the lemongrass.

To prepare the salad, spread the peanuts in a roasting pan, sprinkle with soy sauce, and toast in a preheated oven at 400°F for 10 minutes. Take care, because they burn easily. Remove from the oven, let cool, then crush coarsely with a mortar and pestle.

Grate or thinly slice the papaya and put in a bowl. Add the lime juice, chile, peanuts, and cilantro and mix well.

To finish the curry, heat the safflower oil in a large wok or skillet. When hot, add the bok choy and white cabbage and stir-fry for 3–4 minutes until starting to soften. Add the spinach, bean sprouts, and cilantro. Cook for 1 minute until the spinach has wilted. Add the curry sauce, with salt and pepper to taste, then reheat.

Serve the curry with the rice and salad alongside.

COOK'S TIP

Thai ingredients are readily available in fresh or dried form from large supermarkets and Asian stores. Lemongrass, galangal, ginger, and lime leaves all freeze well if you want to keep some on hand.

butternut squash and goat cheese gratin

with warm parsnip and ginger purée

A lovely dish, beautifully balanced and perfect for an evening at home with friends. Parsnips and ginger are a surprising combination but the sweetness of the parsnips and the warm flavor of the ginger are compelling and an interesting variation on the traditional mashed potato.

4 lb. butternut squash or pumpkin, peeled, seeded, and cut into large chunks

$\frac{1}{4}$ cup olive oil

4 tablespoons unsalted butter, cut into pieces

12 oz. canned corn, drained, or frozen and thawed

$\frac{1}{2}$ teaspoon freshly grated nutmeg

2 garlic cloves, crushed

leaves from 2 sprigs of thyme

sea salt and freshly ground black pepper

3 cups fresh bread crumbs

4 oz. aged goat cheese (Bucheron), crumbled

GINGER AND PARSNIP PURÉE

$1\frac{1}{2}$ lb. parsnips, coarsely chopped

1 tablespoon safflower oil

1 teaspoon ground ginger

$1\frac{1}{4}$ cups heavy cream

sea salt and freshly ground black pepper

watercress, to serve

2 ovenproof glass dishes

a baking tray

SERVES 4

Put the squash in an ovenproof glass dish with 1 tablespoon of the olive oil, the butter, corn, nutmeg, garlic, thyme, salt, and pepper.

To make the topping, mix the bread crumbs, goat cheese, and remaining 3 tablespoons oil in a bowl, then sprinkle over the squash. Cover with foil and bake in a preheated oven at 400°F for 40 minutes. Remove the foil and cook for a further 15 minutes until golden brown on top.

Put the parsnips on a baking tray and sprinkle with salt, safflower oil, and ginger. Roast for about 20 minutes until the parsnips are tender. Transfer to a food processor, add the cream, and blend until smooth. Add salt and pepper to taste. Transfer to the second ovenproof glass dish, cover with foil, and heat in the oven for 10 minutes.

Serve the gratin with the ginger and parsnip purée and a generous bunch of watercress on the side.

roasted sweet potatoes with beet and carrot salad

Peanuts give a creamy richness to sauces. Here, they are complemented by the sweetness of the potato and pineapple juice and offset by a zesty, brightly colored topping. Like most spiced dishes, this will continue to develop in flavor if left overnight, so make it a day ahead. What could be easier?

Put the sweet potatoes on the baking tray and sprinkle with safflower oil and salt. Roast in a preheated oven at 400°F for 30 minutes or until tender.

Meanwhile, to make the sauce, put the onion, chile, ginger, garlic, and paprika in a medium saucepan. Cook over medium heat for 10 minutes until the onion is soft. Stir in the tomatoes, pineapple juice, stock, peanut butter, and soy sauce and continue cooking gently for about 10–15 minutes until the sauce has thickened.

Heat a large wok or skillet and add the spinach. Cook for 1–2 minutes until just wilted, then add the sauce and cooked sweet potatoes. Turn carefully to coat, then keep the pan warm over gentle heat.

To make the salad, put the carrot, beets, lime juice, and soy sauce in a bowl and toss well. Serve the salad and sweet potatoes with couscous and cilantro.

2 lb. sweet potatoes, cut into wedges

1 tablespoon safflower oil

sea salt

8 oz. spinach

SPICY PEANUT SAUCE

1 red onion, thinly sliced

1 red bird chile, finely chopped

1 inch fresh ginger, peeled and grated

1 garlic clove, crushed

1 teaspoon paprika

2 cups canned chopped tomatoes, a 14 oz. can

$^3/_4$ cup pineapple juice

$^3/_4$ cup vegetable stock or water

2 cups organic peanut butter, about 8 oz.

1 tablespoon soy sauce

BEET AND CARROT SALAD

1$^3/_4$ cups grated carrots, about 8 oz.

1$^1/_2$ cups grated raw beets, about 6 oz.

$^1/_4$ cup lime juice

1 tablespoon soy sauce

TO SERVE

1$^1/_2$ cups couscous, prepared according to the method on page 35

chopped cilantro

a baking tray

SERVES 4

rhubarb, ginger, and banana crumble

Crumble is one of those familiar recipes that almost everyone has made at some time in their lives. My version is given a banana twist, which makes a wicked combination with rhubarb, ginger, and crunchy oats in the crumble topping. Serve with crème fraîche, cream, or ice cream for a winning dessert.

Put the rhubarb in a medium saucepan and add the ginger, sugar, and 2 tablespoons water. Bring to a boil and simmer for 7–10 minutes, until the rhubarb has softened. Transfer to a blender and process to a purée. Transfer to the prepared pie dish and top with the bananas and a sprinkling of cinnamon.

To make the topping, put the flour and butter in a bowl and, using your fingertips, rub the butter into the flour until it looks like fine bread crumbs. Add the sugar and two-thirds of the oats. Sprinkle over the fruit mixture and top with the remaining oats. Bake in a preheated oven at 400°F for 30–40 minutes.

Serve hot with crème fraîche or ice cream.

2½ cups chopped rhubarb, about 1 lb.

2 inches fresh ginger, peeled and grated

2 tablespoons sugar

7 medium bananas, thickly cut diagonally

¼ teaspoon ground cinnamon

crème fraîche or ice cream, to serve

OAT TOPPING

¾ cup all-purpose flour

7 tablespoons chilled unsalted butter, cut into cubes

⅔ cup sugar

⅔ cup rolled oats

a pie dish, 10-inches diameter, lightly greased

SERVES 4

index

conversion charts

Weights and measures have been rounded up or down slightly to make measuring easier.

volume equivalents

american	metric	imperial
1 teaspoon	5 ml	
1 tablespoon	15 ml	
¼ cup	60 ml	2 fl.oz.
⅓ cup	75 ml	2½ fl.oz.
½ cup	125 ml	4 fl.oz.
⅔ cup	150 ml	5 fl.oz. (¼ pint)
¾ cup	175 ml	6 fl.oz.
1 cup	250 ml	8 fl.oz.

weight equivalents:

imperial	metric
1 oz.	25 g
2 oz.	50 g
3 oz.	75 g
4 oz.	125 g
5 oz.	150 g
6 oz.	175 g
7 oz.	200 g
8 oz. (½ lb.)	250 g
9 oz.	275 g
10 oz.	300 g
11 oz.	325 g
12 oz.	375 g
13 oz.	400 g
14 oz.	425 g
15 oz.	475 g
16 oz. (1 lb.)	500 g
2 1b.	1 kg

measurements:

inches	cm
¼ inch	5 mm
½ inch	1 cm
¾ inch	1.5 cm
1 inch	2.5 cm
2 inches	5 cm
3 inches	7 cm
4 inches	10 cm
5 inches	12 cm
6 inches	15 cm
7 inches	18 cm
8 inches	20 cm
9 inches	23 cm
10 inches	25 cm
11 inches	28 cm
12 inches	30 cm

oven temperatures:

225°F	110°C	Gas ¼
250°F	120°C	Gas ½
275°F	140°C	Gas 1
300°F	150°C	Gas 2
325°F	160°C	Gas 3
350°F	180°C	Gas 4
375°F	190°C	Gas 5
400°F	200°C	Gas 6
425°F	220°C	Gas 7
450°F	230°C	Gas 8
475°F	240°C	Gas 9